INVITATION TO FOLLOW

Nina

...your company is re...
to celebrate
...elle Rollins' Fortieth B...
...ay, the third of May
...thousand and eight
...o'clock in the evening
...am Road, Northwest
Atlanta

Glen Rollins

Bla...

DINNER ON THE LAWN
SEPTEMBER 23, 2009
Danielle & Glen R...

Danielle Rollins

DANIELLE ROLLINS

PLEASE JOIN M...
FOR A CASUAL LUNC...
IN HONOR OF RACHEL R...

AT HO...
TUESDAY, MA...
1:0...

VILLA SOLEIA
VILLEFRANCHE

SWIMMING

...LD

ASHLEY AND ALAN ARRIVE
9:00 DINNER

...OF AUGUST

...llen and Dan...
...hatham Hal...
3000 Andrews Drive
Atlanta

Georg...

In the presence of
...Princess Anne, The Princess Roy...
President of the Animal...

...anielle
...llins

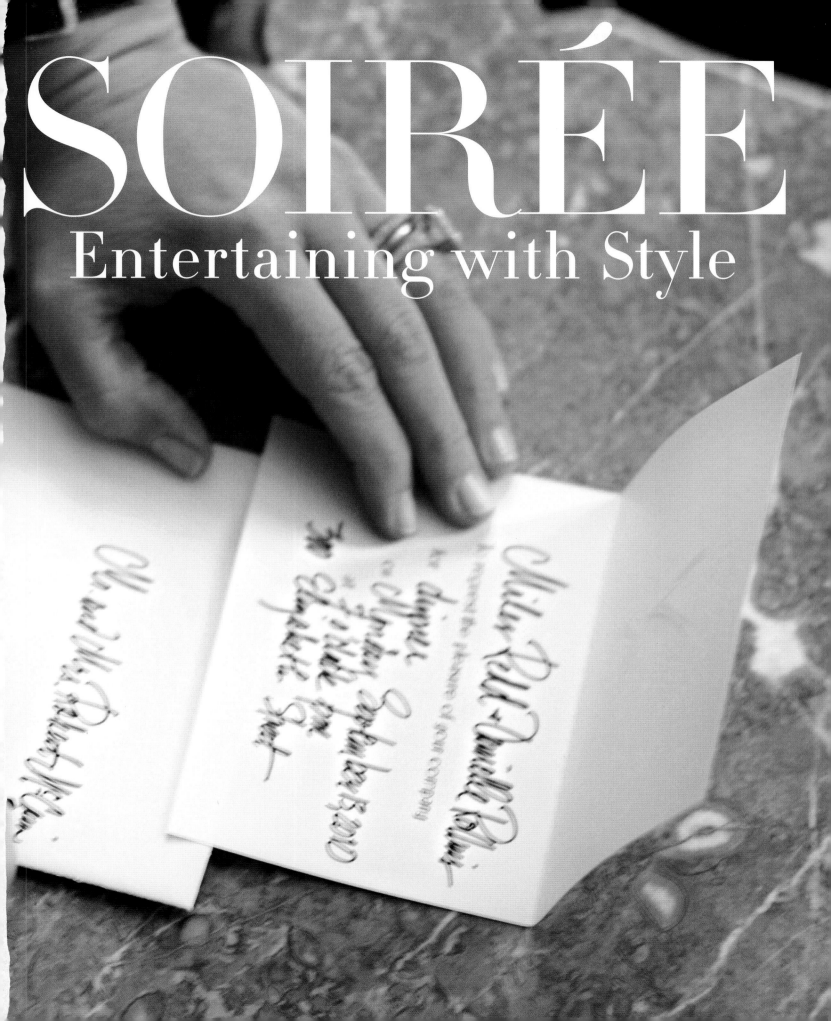

SOIRÉE
Entertaining with Style

SOIRÉE
Entertaining with Style

DANIELLE ROLLINS

RIZZOLI
NEW YORK

New York Paris London Milan

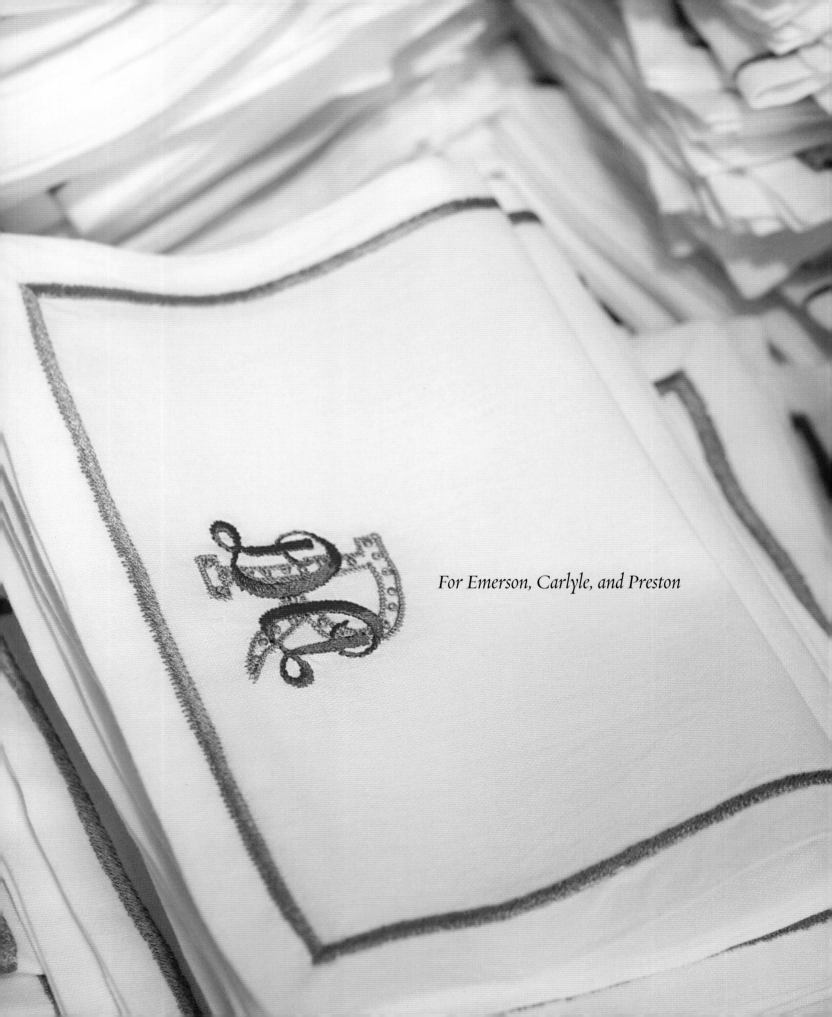

For Emerson, Carlyle, and Preston

CONTENTS

INTRODUCTION

Who would have ever thought that whipping up a soufflé or setting a dazzling table would boost my spirit and give me strength, but it does. I genuinely get energized from hosting parties, large or small. The "lights . . . camera . . . action!" nature of it all makes me happy. From the initial spark of inspiration to the sometimes complicated logistics that it takes to choreograph a fête of any proportion to the final zip of my dress before I head downstairs to greet my guests, there is nothing I enjoy more than throwing a great party. When life gets me down, the fastest way to get back up is to put on a swipe of lipstick and have a little soirée!

Life goes by all too quickly. A little dinner with great friends gives us a chance to create beautiful, lasting memories that we can draw on during life's rough patches. I know as you're reading this you're probably thinking, "I don't have time or energy or all the right things to throw something fabulous together." But you do. And you'll love the gratification you get from having friends over and hearing people laugh along with you.

My middle child was badly injured in an accident and ultimately spent several years recovering. I had an opportunity to host a dinner at my home to honor Oscar de la Renta, when he was in town for a fashion show and personal appearance at Neiman Marcus to benefit Children's Healthcare of Atlanta, the institution that saved my daughter's life. Intimidated by the idea of hosting a dinner for one of my lifelong favorite designers, and feeling a little hesitant about the idea of doing anything at all that had any hint of frivolity, I had a hard time planning. But in going through the motions I actually began to enjoy myself. During the dinner, while looking up and down a long elegant table at all the smiling faces over candlelight, I realized that my true joy was back. And upon reflection it was the gift of others' hospitality that got me through the low points. I had forgotten how great a party could make me feel. And guess who it was that turned to me during that dinner and suggested this book? Yes, that's right, Oscar de la Renta, with the adorable Miles Redd chiming in right behind him before I could even think twice.

You may not be entertaining for a world-class designer, but no matter. The same principles apply to any festivity. Most important, there are no rules. The most valuable thing I've learned, which I hope you take to heart, is that there is no right or wrong way to throw a party. You don't have to have a degree from a culinary school to be a great host or hostess. I have taken cooking lessons, but I have not had training in flower arranging, decorating, or in any related area. All you need is a little passion. Draw on the things in life that inspire you and make you feel good. Entertaining isn't about money or decor or finding the most famous chef in the world to cook for your guests. It's about people. People make the party, period. Creating a fabulous guest list is akin to a fashion designer putting together an amazing outfit for the runway. For me, it's sheer happiness and pride to assemble the perfect crowd. If I love someone, I want the other someones I love to love him or her too.

I also believe in using shortcuts to save time, and in letting others help you do the things you don't have time to do yourself. I know that my guests will enjoy themselves if I do. No one benefits from an exhausted and grumpy hostess! So learn how to make one really great meal that you can use over and over again. If you can't boil water, hire a caterer or get take-out from your favorite restaurant. If you don't bake, buy a tremendously great tart from a bakery; you can serve it with freshly made whipped cream to give it some flair. If you are too intimidated to arrange your own flowers, use a simple bowl of fruit or go see your local florist.

At a party, people cherish the personal touches, the relaxed time together, and the creation of traditions—it's about making your guests feel special. Adding personal details—handwriting names on place cards, arranging thoughtful seating assignments for a dinner party, placing fresh flowers on the table, garnishing glasses of water with mint sprigs, using your china and cloth napkins for even the simplest gathering—creates unforgettable moments.

That's what this book is about, creating moments that we can share and cherish. It's about making it easy on yourself when you do entertain and about spreading a little joy in life to maximize the ups and minimize the downs. I hope even reading this puts a smile on your face. It was a thrill for me to put it together. So, bon appétit and cheers for your next very own soirée!

THE ESSENCE OF ENTERTAINING

Essence comes from the Greek expression that means *tí esti,* literally "what it is." I start here when planning—what is it I want to accomplish? What kind of party do I want to hold? The essence of a gathering doesn't just happen; it is planned and created with loving effort.

INVITATIONS

Invitations should create a sense of excitement as well as hint at what is in store, whether it is a theme or feeling. An upbeat invitation literally jumps out from among the piles of junk mail and bills and will inspire the recipient to go all out, knowing it will be a great soirée!

Unusual and festive invitations for inspiration include custom "fortunes" placed inside fortune cookies in a Chinese takeout box; a colorful fan revealing the invitation's wording when unfolded; a CD of music with the invitation on it; photos of the guest of honor, particularly from childhood, or of the location if it is a destination party; a sombrero or cowboy hat with the invitation tied around the crown; a Mason jar with the invitation on a recipe card; sumptuous calligraphy in a beautiful shade of ink thermographed or engraved on colored cardstock with contrasting paper lining the envelope . . .

Personally I never like guessing what to wear, so I try to be very specific with my guests: Bonfire Chic for a cozy autumn outdoor gathering, Denim and Diamonds for a boot-scootin' barbeque, Barefoot and Black Tie for a formal party on the beach. Or give guests a color guideline, such as, for example, pink and white tea-party attire.

Don't overlook the stamps. Photo images creating custom stamps that cleverly tie in with the theme make an envelope pop! Hand delivering invitations is an over-the-top gesture that's sure to get attention.

MUSIC

Music sets the tone for a party. A bluegrass trio sounds festive for a barbecue, a small chamber ensemble sets a sophisticated tone for a quiet dinner, and DJs mean lively after-dinner fun. Your choice of music should always seem deliberate. Don't pick something just because you like it—it should fit the mood of your event. During cocktails, I like guests to get into the party spirit, so I play music that is upbeat in tempo. During dinner, music should fade away and become a subtle part of the background, allowing the dinner conversation to be the predominant sound. And when dessert is served, a return to more lively music is a good way to get the

ABOVE AND OPPOSITE: An invitation sets the mood and tone for any party. Assembling invitations to be hand delivered helped me get in the party spirit ahead of time! Planning a party is just as much fun sometimes as the actual party!

blood flowing again! If you're lucky, this can result in a little late-night impromptu dancing. In general, music should be loud enough to be heard, but not loud enough for karaoke. (Unless you want to do karaoke, in which case by all means crank up the music and let your friends sing with reckless abandon!)

For larger parties, cocktails-only gatherings, or outdoor gatherings, live music is perfect because it becomes a focal point of the event. Consider hiring a piano player to play jazz standards or Christmas carol sing-alongs. On a budget? A talented young high school or college student might be willing to play for a nominal fee to help add experience on a resume. A calypso, steel band, or reggae group is perfect for a summer gathering at the beach. A banjo player or bluegrass trio suits a pig roast or barbeque.

I prefer a DJ to a cover band because a DJ has the ability to play a wider variety of music, and he or she can adapt to the mood of the crowd, in both volume and rhythm. A DJ can play theme-appropriate music in keeping with the same feel of the rest of the evening. Before hiring, make sure you hear the DJ play a live set, and that he or she has the type of music you want. When planning an outdoor event, check your local sound ordinances or at least warn your neighbors (a note on a box of cookies delivered with the warning can do wonders to sweeten up any potential problem). Make sure you have power in the area you plan to set up.

marbles to the water (a modern look), or cranberries in winter or citrus fruit halves in the summer. Or wrap the containers in fabric or tropical leaves.

A few great garden picks include evergreens or non-blooming plants such as boxwoods, herbs, or ferns, which make a beautiful contrast to a busy table scheme; hydrangeas, orchids, azaleas, or any flowering plant, with pebbles, floral moss, or sphagnum moss to hide the dirt; and blossoms of carnations or roses mounded in a dome shape, easily accomplished by using floral foam in an opaque container. There's no need to get hooked only on flowers: bowls of a single fruit, like bunches and bunches of grapes or fresh summer peaches, create your own version of a Dutch still-life arrangement. Trays of wheatgrass can have a very glamorous visual impact.

LIGHTING

Never underestimate the impact of proper lighting on a party. The lighting sets the tone for your "stage" and creates a dramatic backdrop. However, you don't need a Broadway crew to show up and light your house for you. Put dimmers on light switches and lamps and skip the overhead brights altogether. Low lighting makes us all look good, especially candlelight. Keep the candles scentless indoors and only lightly fragrant if you're outside, because you don't want the smell of the candles to trump the aroma of the food. Mix different-sized candles and be creative with the holders. Outdoors, string lights from trees or use Asian paper lanterns. Hurricanes lanterns can serve as both light and decoration. Or take indoor elements outside and use silver candelabras for an outdoor table. Remember, it's important to be careful with open flames, especially those that are set low to the ground and where people will be walking, so no glam dresses catch fire.

FLOWERS AND DECORATION

Flowers just make people happy. I feel that flowers or something from nature are critical to entertaining. If you're on a budget, buy masses of carnations or other inexpensive flowers rather than something more expensive of which you can only afford a small amount. More is more, and abundance is always the way to go! Also, stick with seasonal plants and flowers, rather than expensive or exotic flowers.

Using the flowers and greenery from my own yard and garden keeps my arrangements seasonal and casual. I am a strong believer in the idea that entertaining in your home should never look overdone or contrived. By using your own vases, pots, and containers—including those that are repurposed or nontraditional—there will be a synergy between the expression of your own personality and your home décor.

Floral foam can be a great help if the vase isn't transparent. If you use solid containers all you see are the flowers, not the stems. Floral tape is also useful: Tape a grid over the top of the vase, starting in the center with the taller flowers and working your way out. It's helpful to do flowers at eye level so that you can see what they will look like to the guests when seated. Another useful tidbit: For transparent containers, cover flower stems by adding

OPPOSITE PAGE: *Large vases of Limelight hydrangeas created a visual draw to the bar at the end of the lawn, beckoning guests down for a drink. Mixologists created specialty cocktails listed on a drink menu elegantly framed in heirloom silver, while William Yeoward hurricanes and mixed linens on the tables added just the right amount of juxtaposed formality and scale to the setting and feel of the party. A bar is always the gathering point at any party, so why not make it part of the decoration?*

BUILDING A BAR AND
SETTING THE TABLE

Creating an attractive bar as a focal point makes any party stand out; it is the gathering place where most people end up almost immediately at a party. Simply put: The bar says, "Welcome to my party! Please relax and enjoy yourself." As the bar is a place to stroll up to and strike up a conversation with someone you don't know, it's a starting point for a great evening. A pretty bowl or container holding snacks will make waiting for a drink more pleasant. Run-of-the-mill popcorn jazzed up with spices or Parmesan cheese makes an ideal bar snack. Serve one special drink or a small selection rather than have an open bar.

To create a stunning bar, cover a table with fabric, layered or otherwise, and don't get stressed about using the perfectly sized tablecloth. Use what you happen to have in your home: burlap, old curtains, or even sheets. Mix and match and use pins to pinch to the right fit. Cloth napkins always add elegance, but they don't have to be elaborately embroidered linen ones; making them out of bandanas, inexpensive gingham, or any fabric is a good investment since you can reuse them again and again.

Think outside the box for glassware, too: Mason jars for cocktails, Moroccan tea glasses for Champagne, Venetian glass picked up on holiday for water glasses—and look for after-holiday sales to stock up on festively colored ones. You don't have to use a glass just for its intended use. Be creative.

Delightful garnishes can take a bar from ordinary to fantastic. I like paper straws in fanciful colors displayed in a colorful glass, a small terra-cotta pot, or a silver julep cup; cranberries, kumquats, blueberries, or tomatoes on long bamboo skewers; crystallized ginger, candied citrus peel, sugared flowers, or fresh flowers; thinly sliced citrus wheels or thick citrus zests made with a carrot peeler; herbs, fruit, or flowers frozen in ice cubes or oddly shaped ice cubes. Proper bar tools will simplify things even if the cocktails are premade, so make sure your bar area is stocked with jiggers, muddlers, stirrers, juicers, shakers, and blenders for frozen drinks (I like Waring and Vitamix).

How you set up tables for dining creates the overall tableaux of your party. You can mix and match silver, place settings, fabrics, colors, and centerpieces as long as there is some coordinating theme. Your goal is to create a sense of fantasy and magic, not perfection. Sometimes a good plan is to create nifty little corners for intimate dining; sometimes one long, communal table in a larger space is the best bet. The choices are infinite. Again—no rules! Just choose your theme, go with what you've got, and be creative. Hospitality is the ability to make people feel welcomed and appreciated.

FOOD AND MENU PLANNING

Like everything else on party night, the food should fit the theme, setting, and mood of the night. Keep it simple and use seasonal, fresh ingredients whenever possible. I don't like overly complicated menus or dishes. When you're the famous chef of the night, do as much prep ahead of time as possible. Simplify your life! Using premade or purchased items for parts of your menu will give you more time to enjoy your own party rather than having to be in the kitchen all day. Have lasagnas from a local restaurant made in your own dishes, or serve homemade cookies with store-bought ice cream, or add fresh whipped cream to a pie picked up from a favorite bakery. This little extra effort is always appreciated.

Stick with go-to recipes you've done before and always be prepared for Plan B. You might burn something or mess up a recipe, but that's not a party ender. Keeping a well-stocked pantry and a few items in the freezer for emergency improvisation is a secret that anyone who loves to entertain knows. Some of my most memorable and successful dinner parties have been spur-of-the-moment decisions or the result of a near failure!

When you're entertaining, you need to think "abundance," so if that means inviting fewer people in order to be able to serve better-quality food, then adjust the guest list accordingly. Nobody should leave feeling hungry. Also, remember that the guests won't be eating the flowers, so put the majority of your budget toward the food. Whether it's a buffet or passed trays of hors d'oeuvres, keep the platters full and fresh, because nobody ever wants to the take the last one of anything, and empty platters look messy. A buffet table is one of the focal points and part of the overall decoration of the party, so it is imperative that it look as good at the end of the party as it did at the beginning. To ensure it stays attractive throughout the event, always have an extra dish ready for rotation to replace a container that is less than three quarters full.

Great wine makes a party more enjoyable and encourages the guests to linger longer. That doesn't mean an expensive wine; like everything else you're serving, think "abundance." Work with a local wine store to find regional wines to suit your menu and your budget.

CATERING

A comfortable professional relationship with your caterers is critical. Look for someone who seems able to grasp the tone, mood, and needs of your party. If they can only do a standard list of things and are not willing to tailor a menu to your needs, they might not be the best caterers for you.

Have them to the house ahead of time to see how you live and where everything is. Make sure you're both clear on what you'll provide and what they're in charge of delivering, as well as the overall feel of the event. Good caterers should be able to improvise and not be disruptive. It is imperative to have someone with a high standard of service because your job is to entertain your guests—and the caterers' job is to give you the freedom to allow that to happen. The day of, have a pre-party meeting with the staff and give detailed directions: I always ask that no empty glasses, crumpled napkins, or empty serving dishes be left sitting around. Make sure to agree on a budget ahead of time so there are no misunderstandings, and on the day of your event, fill envelopes with tips so you can hand them to the caterers at the end of a successful evening. And whether you are cooking or having a catered event, try to make the food feel homey, not as if it is part of a Vegas buffet.

No matter what you do, do it with graciousness! Mix a sense of humor with a dash of effort and remember that the devil is in the details and the payoff will be a spectacular soirée. Hospitality should give as much joy to the host or the hostess as to the guests who are lucky enough to receive the invitations. Relax and don't try to impress people; rather focus on connecting with them and creating memories. After all, it is just a party, and entertaining should be fun!

OPPOSITE: *Setting out as many things as possible ahead of a party saves time and helps to ensure a smooth set-up, especially if you are using a caterer. A sample place setting and visual walk through lets the caterer know exactly how I envision the table and shows me if I am missing anything. Post-It notes on all the items specify which course each item is to be used for.* LEFT: *Pounding bags of ice with the flat side of a hammer is a quick and easy way to get crushed ice!*

A CLASSIC DINNER PARTY

Serves 8

GIN-GIN MULE **

SALADS OF MUSHROOMS WITH CORIANDER;
CELERY ROOT REMOULADE; ASPARAGUS, ENDIVE,
CUCUMBER, AND TOMATOES WITH VINAIGRETTE

GRILLED DOVER SOLE WITH SPINACH PUREE
AND MUSTARD HOLLANDAISE **

BUTTERED PARSLEY POTATOES **

RASPBERRY SOUFFLÉ **

TEA AND MACARONS

KEEP CHIC AND CARRY ON

Miles Redd, an interior decorator and man-about-town, loves a dash of glamour. Last summer, to celebrate our friendship, he and I hosted a small black-tie dinner party in his uber-chic Manhattan townhouse, with Miles dictating the evening's theme as Paris in the '50s. Small black-tie dinner parties at home may seem a thing of the past, but if you give your guests forewarning they will enjoy the opportunity to dress to the nines, which always creates a festive atmosphere. We set up an outdoor dinner for eight on the terrace, where an oasis of crisp boxwood, French blue treillage, and clipped hornbeam trees in Versailles boxes disguised a not-so-Parisian view.

PREVIOUS PAGES: *Matching blue seat cushions with white piping united a group of mixed metal chairs surrounding a stone table, all perched on a harlequin-patterned wood floor. In keeping with the mood of vintage elegance, the table was covered in Dior gray duchesse satin and an overlay of white linen embroidered with sheaths of wheat, a flea market find, along with hotel silver and antique china. In entertaining, just as in decorating, a mix of old and new creates visual interest and gives guests a feeling of comfort.* OPPOSITE AND ABOVE: *The flowers were inspired by the soft arrangements of the 1950s, dahlias and roses in tones of pink and coral mixed with feathery ferns, while small antique tennis trophies held individual bunches of stephanotis.*

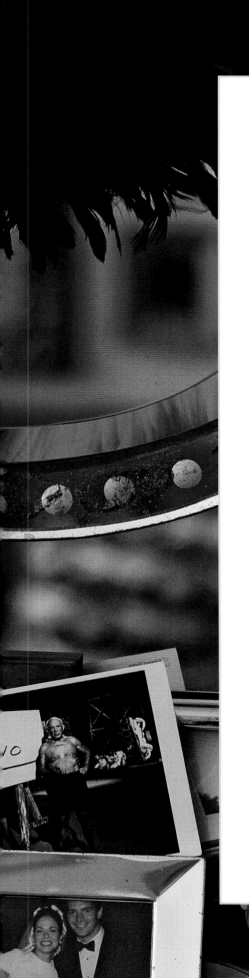

As I prepared a Gin-Gin Mule, a classic drink from The Carlyle Hotel's famed Bemelmans Bar, and poured it into a silver julep cup to keep it cold, I heard a deafening thunderclap, which was followed by an unexpected downpour. Miles's nephew gallantly shielded me with an umbrella as I rushed to rescue the linens, dishes, and flowers. My motto is "Keep Calm and Carry On" (borrowed from the posters adorning Great Britain's subways during World War II), and when Mother Nature doesn't share your party spirit there is really nothing to do but have a sense of humor and move to Plan B. So, after fortifying ourselves with a Gin-Gin Mule—it's important to test the cocktails pre-party!—Miles and I quickly reset for dinner indoors in a record thirty minutes. By the time guests arrived through the living room's zebra-hide-upholstered doors, a delightful mix of cocktail standards were playing on the iPod dock as we relaxed on his Vreeland red silk velvet sofa.

After a leisurely paced cocktail "hour-plus" (Miles warns never to rush this part of the evening), guests ventured upstairs, none the wiser to the earlier scramble and delighted to have dinner in the host's bathroom. Come again? Mind you this is no ordinary bathroom: the impossibly glamorous all-mirrored space, designed by legendary architect David Adler, was retrofitted from the Armour Estate in Chicago and is the largest room in the house.

Knowing when to delegate, we had Pascal Lorange, of Fig & Olive, prepare Dover sole, buttered potatoes with parsley, and pureed spinach, followed by a raspberry soufflé. Miles and I pitched in to help serve dinner, ensuring the flight of stairs didn't create a slowdown. Tea with macaroons after dinner kept the conversation flowing, and guests lingered comfortably for an end-of-summer soirée worthy of 1950s social swans Babe Paley and Slim Keith.

PREVIOUS PAGES: *Things were pulled from Miles's well-stocked entertaining closet of gathered treasures and made the table settings feel very personal.*
THIS PAGE: *A group of highly personal family photographs, postcards, and the occasional object create a curious jumble when collected on Miles's mantle, a romantic, Edwardian touch in this modern age.*

GIN-GIN MULE

8 ounces ginger simple syrup (recipe opposite)
8 ounces freshly squeezed lime juice (8-10 limes)
16 ounces gin
8 ounces ginger beer
16 sprigs fresh mint (8 for muddling and 8 for garnish)
8 pieces candied ginger (optional, for garnish)
8 highball glasses and enough crushed ice to fill them

In a large pitcher, combine ginger simple syrup, freshly
squeezed lime juice, gin, and ginger beer and stir. Muddle a
mint sprig in the bottom of each glass. Fill each glass with
crushed ice then Gin-Gin mixture, adding a bit more ginger
beer if you prefer the drink a little less tart or more lime juice
as needed if you prefer a bit more tangy. Garnish drinks with
a sprig of mint and a piece of candied ginger on the rim of
the glass. Serve immediately with a straw.

GINGER SIMPLE SYRUP
1 large piece of fresh ginger, peeled and sliced in half
1 cup sugar

1. Combine 1 cup water and sugar in a saucepan. Bring to a
   boil, stirring constantly until sugar dissolves and the liquid
   becomes clear. Reduce heat and simmer, stirring continuously, for 5 to 10 minutes.

2. Remove from heat and add fresh ginger. Let cool to room
   temperature then strain liquid into a container, discarding the
   ginger. Syrup will keep in the refrigerator for up to 2 weeks.

PREVIOUS PAGES: *I decided to wear a vintage Oscar de la
Renta confection with layers of tulle net with sequins.
Miles said it was "Grace Kelly meets Prince Ranier."*
ABOVE AND OPPOSITE: *Neither Miles nor I are one bit shy
about specifying our guests' attire—after all, people are part of
the backdrop of a party and their dress adds to the mood.*

GRILLED DOVER SOLE WITH SPINACH PUREE AND MUSTARD HOLLANDAISE

8 Dover sole fillets
1 tablespoon extra-virgin olive oil
Sea salt and freshly ground black pepper

1. Preheat an outdoor grill or grill pan to medium. While it is preheating, rinse fish and pat dry. When the grill is hot, oil the rack. Brush sole on both sides with olive oil and season with salt and pepper to taste.

2. Grill fillets 4 to 5 minutes on each side, making sure temperature is low to moderate, as sole is very delicate. Serve immediately with Spinach Puree and Mustard Hollandaise Sauce.

SPINACH PUREE

8 bunches fresh spinach
2 tablespoons extra-virgin olive oil, plus more for garnish
Sea salt and freshly ground black pepper

1. Wash and dry spinach. Heat 2 tablespoons olive oil in a large pan over medium heat. Add spinach and sauté just until tender; do not overcook.

2. Puree sautéed spinach in a food processor and season with salt and pepper; drizzle more oil over the spinach to taste once it is plated.

MUSTARD HOLLANDAISE SAUCE

1½ cups unsalted butter
5 egg yolks
Sea salt and freshly ground black pepper
1½ tablespoons freshly squeezed lemon juice (about ½ lemon)
1 tablespoon Dijon mustard

1. Fill a saucepan with water 2 inches deep and place over medium heat. Melt butter in another saucepan, making sure to take it off the heat as soon as it has melted.

2. Put the egg yolks and 1 tablespoon water in a bowl that will sit easily on top of the saucepan of water. When the water in the saucepan is steaming, place the bowl on top of the saucepan and whisk the yolks and water rapidly and constantly until the mixture thickens, making sure to scrape the sides of the bowl with the whisk so that no yolk sticks to the bowl.

3. When the mixture thickens, remove the pan with the yolk mixture from the heat and slowly and steadily whisk in the melted butter to incorporate. The sauce should be homogenized, not greasy. Once the butter is completely incorporated into the egg yolks, season with salt, pepper, lemon juice, and mustard to taste. Put the hollandaise in a container that can fit inside another container of warm water and set aside until ready to serve. Note: Do not use hollandaise that is more than 2½ hours old.

PREVIOUS PAGES: *Since Mother Nature rained on our party but not our party spirit, a quick change of venue allowed the party to go on as planned. Small spaces don't mean you can't entertain; you just need to think through how to do it well. Keeping the guest count to a number you can comfortably accommodate in multiple situations makes for a relaxed host and means no fuss if something has to be changed at the last minute.* OPPOSITE: *Place cards were single gardenia blooms, with the guests' names written on the leaves in silver ink. The gardenias were placed on top of postcards featuring Richard Avedon photographs of 1950s models. On the back of the postcards we had written, "Strike the same pose!" This created a great icebreaker to thaw that initial awkwardness upon seating. When people don't know each other well, it is a good idea to have a way to create interaction—and humor is always appreciated.*

BUTTERED PARSLEY POTATOES

36 to 40 baby fingerling potatoes
1 bunch flat-leaf parsley
½ cup unsalted butter
Sea salt and freshly ground black pepper

1. Peel potatoes. Wash, dry, and chop parsley.

2. Place potatoes in a large pot with two large pinches of salt
   and cover with water; boil potatoes until fork tender.
   Drain and mix potatoes gently with parsley and butter.
   Season with salt and pepper to taste.

RASPBERRY SOUFFLÉ

1 tablespoon butter, for the dishes
8 tablespoons sugar, plus more for the dishes
9 large eggs
4 tablespoons all-purpose flour
1 teaspoon vanilla extract
2 cups whole milk
Raspberry Sauce

1. Preheat oven to 400°F. Butter 8 small soufflé dishes and
   lightly dust the insides with 2 tablespoons of sugar.

2. Separate eggs, being careful not to get any yolk in the
   whites. Place 6 yolks in one bowl and 3 yolks in another
   bowl. Reserve egg whites in another bowl.

3. Mix 6 yolks with 3 tablespoons of the sugar, the flour, and
   vanilla. Heat milk in a pan, and, whisking rapidly, add the
   yolk-sugar-flour mixture. Boil until thick, then remove
   from heat. Slowly, so eggs won't scramble, add remaining
   3 egg yolks, stirring to combine.

4. Beat egg whites in a large bowl with the remaining 3
   tablespoons sugar until stiff peaks form. (When you run
   the whisk through the whites, they should stand like a
   mountain range and not fall back down.) Carefully fold
   egg whites into the pan of milk and yolks, stirring rapidly
   to combine. Swirl in ½ cup Raspberry Sauce, reserving the
   rest for garnish. Using a spatula, pour the batter into the
   prepared soufflé dishes.

5. Bake 25 to 35 minutes or until top forms a perfect dome.
   Gently remove from oven and serve immediately with
   remaining Raspberry Sauce.

RASPBERRY SAUCE
½ cup sugar
1 pint fresh raspberries

1. Combine ¼ cup water and sugar in a medium saucepan
   and bring to a boil. Remove from heat and let cool.

2. Pour sugar-water mixture into a blender; add raspberries.
   Blend until smooth, then strain through a mesh colander
   over a bowl and reserve.

OPPOSITE: *After dinner, guests retreated to Miles's living room
for tea and macarons and a spirited post-dinner conversation
with plenty of laughter.* ABOVE: *A decadent raspberry soufflé
topped with raspberry sauce and fresh raspberries was a perfect
finishing touch to a classic dinner party.*

WINTER SUPPER PARTY

Serves 8

Tamarind Margaritas **

Shad Roe with Scrambled Duck Eggs

Crab Samosa with Truffle Mayonnaise **

Spanish Mackerel with Amaranth,
Cashews, and Brussels Sprouts **

Braised Capon Cavatelli with Whipped Ricotta **

Lela's Biscotti and Gold-Dusted Vanilla Ice Cream **

TWO TEXANS ENTERTAIN WITH STYLE

Lela Rose, a fellow Texan and fashion designer, lives in a six-thousand-square-foot ground-floor storefront in Tribeca with her husband, Brandon Jones, and her two children. With nods to her home state, the floors are done in mesquite wood, and a large vase in the living room holds tall branches of cotton bolls. She and I share a love of living with gusto, entertaining for sheer pleasure, and doing things in a big way, which just goes to show that you can take the girls out of Texas, but you can't take the Texan out of the girls!

The morning of the party, Lela and I hopped on her custom-built rickshaw bike and headed to the florist Fisher & Page in the flower market. We settled on succulents since their architectural shapes were a perfect fit with Lela's aesthetic approach to modern design. Small enough to fit on the narrow tables, they had a purple-green hue that nicely offset the muted jewel-tone quilts Lela had brought home from a recent trip to India. Since she is quite handy with a needle and thread, she simply stitched them all together to create one long table covering.

PREVIOUS PAGE: *Lela and I took great care setting the table to make sure it looked attractive both when standing and when sitting down.* ABOVE (CLOCKWISE FROM TOP LEFT): *Flowers picked up early on the morning of the party in Lela's custom rickshaw bike started off the festivities for both of us. Stitch, Lela's beloved dog, and I were loaded to the max as Lela peddled us back to her loft, with the Empire State Building providing a movie-worthy New York backdrop. Guests always appreciate a little take-home memory. The Peter Sellers movie* The Party *was a perfect memento of a madcap evening. Teal menu cards handwritten in silver ink in the hostess's handwriting matched perfectly and kept with the organic feel of the table settings.*

Lela and Brandon's apartment has two incredible concealed dining tables. At the flip of a switch, one long table rises up from within the floor, while another switch allows a glass table to descend from the ceiling. Together they become one seemingly endless table as needed, yet they can be stored efficiently and invisibly away when not in use.

We did a quick sweep around the apartment to gather plates, platters, glasses, linens, and everything else we needed and set them out in one place. We tried out a few table settings and decided a mix of different sets of china was in order. After we had set up the basics of the place settings we were able to take a step back to edit and add elements where needed to achieve the perfect mix of height and scale. There is an art to setting a table so it looks pleasing to the eye but leaves enough space for everyone to have a little elbow room to dine comfortably. In this case, we added "Alice in Wonderland" pottery pieces mixed with bright turquoise tapers I had grabbed earlier in the day from the newly opened French candle shop Cire Trudon. From one of the concealed closets nearby, Lela pulled out a stack of charcoal-gray cashmere stadium seats that she uses as her dining room chairs and set them at the end of the table for guests to grab before dinner.

Chef Akhtar Newab, of the restaurant La Esquina, and a close friend of Lela's, arrived midafternoon and efficiently began working on an incredible menu of what we cheerfully deemed "Tex-Mex meets Indian Fusion." Lela is one of the most adventurous and enthusiastic eaters I know, and the menu reflected her creative knack for combining flavors and foods.

An assemblage of "yours, mine, and ours" guests arrived, with the ladies mostly attired in Lela Rose creations, some in the same color, but

OPPOSITE: *The succulent's delicate edges mimicked the ruffled plates' edges. Jewel tones predominated the evening's table settings. Each lady had a delightful hot pink lotus at her place setting. Frances Palmer's whimsical "Alice in Wonderland" candle holders added a nod of playfulness to the table.*

TAMARIND MARGARITAS

8 tablespoons tamarind paste
8 ounces water
16 ounces tequila
8 ounces freshly squeezed lime juice (8 to 10 limes)
8 ounces Cointreau
½ cup honey
2 oranges
Coarse sugar for glass rims
8 margarita glasses filled with ice

1. Dissolve tamarind paste in water in a saucepan over medium heat, stirring constantly until fully dissolved, about 20 minutes. Strain liquid into a container and refrigerate until ready to use.

2. Mix tequila, lime juice, and Cointreau together in a pitcher. Add honey to taste and stir to dissolve.

3. Grate orange zest into sugar in a bowl. Cut zested orange into wedges, cutting away pith, and use to wet each glass rim. Dip each rim into zest and sugar mixture. Fill each glass three quarters full and top with tamarind concentrate; do not stir.

luckily none in the same design, and all wearing extremely high heels. I borrowed a Taffin topaz teardrop necklace from Lela to top off my vintage jumpsuit—remember that when you are seated, your fellow guests will only see you from the waist up, so having a little zing is important!

Guests mixed and mingled in the living room with the windows open both to the street and passing foot traffic, who had no idea that a party was going on just a few feet away from them. The guests were delighted to feel as if they were invisible participants in a Barneys store window display!

Following cocktails, Lela flipped the switch for the glass table and it appeared to float down from the ceiling effortlessly, suspended on industrial steel cables. This "magic" certainly qualified as dinner theater! As with any party, seating is always key, so we put a lot of thought into who sat where and with whom, wanting our friends to mingle. We put the guy who worked at Goldman Sachs next to the girl writing a book about the company and left it all up in the air—will it work or won't it? Any good host or hostess will attest that sometimes a little friction is what keeps a party spirited!

And a spirited party is often marked by a little mischief—in this case a memorable midnight bike ride around the neighborhood. As guests said good-byes we thanked them for coming to our midwinter dinner with take-home gifts of the Peter Sellers movie *The Party*, which couldn't have been a more appropriate gift.

PREVIOUS PAGES (CLOCKWISE FROM TOP LEFT): *Honey was the secret ingredient in tangy tamarind margaritas. Conversations came to a halt as the fully set glass table descended from the ceiling—a real show stopper! Cotton bolls held in a tall vase were cleverly used instead of flowers, as a witty nod to our shared home city, Dallas, where college football is played in the Cotton Bowl.* OPPOSITE: *A quick glance backward helps Lela gage the feel of the party, checking to make sure all the guests have arrived and determine when seating for dinner would be optimal.*

4. To serve, divide arugula and heart of palm evenly among plates. Place a puff pastry barquette on each plate; spoon some of the crab mixture on top, and top with a spoonful of Truffle Mayonnaise and another puff pastry barquette.

TRUFFLE MAYONNAISE

1 (4-ounce) can winter truffle pieces with juice
1 (1-ounce) black winter truffles, minced
1 anchovy fillet (packed in salt), rinsed and minced
3 large eggs
3 tablespoons Champagne vinegar
1½ cups olive oil
½ cup grapeseed oil

1. In a medium-sized pot, combine truffle pieces and juice, black winter truffles, and anchovy. Reduce slowly over low heat until ¼ cup liquid remains. Reserve.

2. Bring a pot of water to a boil; add eggs and cook 5 minutes. Cool eggs in ice water, then peel and chop them. Place eggs and vinegar in bowl of a food processor; slowly add the oils until an emulsion begins to form. Continue until all the oil is added. Transfer to a bowl and fold in truffle mixture. Mayonnaise will be very thick, but it will thin out once the truffle mixture is added.

CRAB SAMOSA WITH TRUFFLE MAYONNAISE

1 pound peekytoe lump crab, picked over
  and any shells discarded
2 leeks, diced, white only, blanched until tender
¼ cup minced chives
2 tablespoons olive oil
Sea salt
1 (17.3-ounce) package puff pastry, thawed
2 cups arugula
1 (8-inch) piece fresh heart of palm, thinly sliced
Truffle Mayonnaise (see recipe below)

1. Gently toss crab, leeks, chives, and oil together in a large bowl. Add salt to taste. Refrigerate until ready to use.

2. Preheat oven to 350°F.

3. Cut a sheet of puff pastry into eight 4-by-8-inch rectangles (called barquettes). Place on a baking sheet lined with parchment paper. Bake, covered with another baking sheet, until fully cooked, 10 to 15 minutes. Set aside to cool.

SPANISH MACKEREL WITH AMARANTH, CASHEWS, AND BRUSSELS SPROUTS

2 pounds Spanish mackerel fillets, skin on
Sea salt and freshly ground black pepper
6 tablespoons plus 2 teaspoons olive oil
3 cups amaranth
4 tomatoes
3 tablespoons minced shallot
⅓ cup roasted cashews
1 clove garlic, pressed or grated
1 cup sugar
1 lemon, sliced paper-thin
1 tablespoon unsalted butter
3 Brussels sprouts

1. Trim ends of mackerel to produce square edges; reserve in refrigerator until ready to use.

2. Bring 10 cups salted water to a boil and add 4 tablespoons oil and amaranth. Cook over medium heat until tender. Strain and rinse under cold water. Drain on a paper-towel-lined baking sheet.

8. Season mackerel with salt and pepper to taste. In a heavy pan, heat butter in a large pan over medium-high heat until it is foaming. Add the mackerel, skin side down, and cook until skin is crisp, about 5 minutes. Turn and cook about 2 minutes more or until medium-rare. Set mackerel on paper towels to drain.

9. Cut ends from Brussels sprouts and peel individual leaves off. Wash leaves and dry. Heat 2 teaspoons oil in a pan over high heat; quickly sauté leaves.

10. To serve, spoon about 3 tablespoons amaranth salad on each plate and add mackerel on top. Place two slices of lemon confit on mackerel to garnish and drizzle about 1 teaspoon of the lemon-infused olive oil around the edge of the plate to accent the food. Serve with Brussel sprouts leaves as the side.

BRAISED CAPON CAVATELLI WITH WHIPPED RICOTTA

1 cup sugar
1 cup sea salt
1 (7-pound) capon
2 carrots, peeled and halved
2 onions, peeled and quartered
2 celery stalks, halved
4 cloves garlic
4 tablespoons olive oil
10 tomatoes, seeds removed, diced
4 rosemary sprigs
4 thyme sprigs
4 quarts chicken stock
½ cup ricotta
2 cups cavatelli pasta
2 tablespoons butter
1 tablespoon Urfa biber (smoked dried Turkish pepper), plus more for garnish
½ cup grated Piave cheese

1. Combine sugar, salt, and 2 gallons cool water in a very large container; do not use aluminum or cast iron. Add capon, and cover and refrigerate overnight (up to 14 hours).

2. Mince carrots, onions, celery, and garlic in a food processor.

3. Preheat oven to 250°F.

4. Bring 6 cups water to a boil and add tomatoes. Cook for 25 seconds, then shock in a bowl of ice water. Peel skin off tomatoes and cut into quarters. Place tomatoes on a baking sheet lined with parchment paper and drizzle with 2 tablespoons oil. Season with salt and pepper to taste.

5. Bake 50 minutes. Remove. When tomatoes are dry and cool, coarsely chop.

6. In a large bowl, combine amaranth, cashews, 2 tablespoons oil, garlic, and tomatoes. Season with sea salt to taste and toss to combine.

7. Preheat oven to 175°F. Bring sugar, 3 tablespoons salt, and 3 cups water to a boil. Lay lemon slices in a flat ovenproof container and pour water, sugar, and salt mixture over the slices. Cover with parchment paper and bake 10 minutes or until tender. Remove lemon slices and transfer them to a lidded container. Pour 2 teaspoons olive oil over lemon slices and store, covered, for up to 2 weeks.

3. Make soffritto by heating 1 tablespoon oil in a large pot over low heat. Add minced vegetables and cook, stirring occasionally, about 10 minutes; add tomatoes and cook, stirring occasionally, for 1 hour. Tie herbs together with kitchen twine and add to soffritto. Cook, stirring often, for 45 minutes.

4. Preheat oven to 350°F.

5. Remove capon from brine; pat dry and roast in the oven until just cooked, about 45 minutes. Once cooled, pull meat from bones and add to the soffritto. Cover with stock and braise 2 hours over low heat to make capon ragù.

6. Add ricotta to a food processor and whip for 30 seconds. Slowly add remaining 3 tablespoons oil and whip until smooth and shiny; reserve.

7. Bring 8 quarts salted water to a boil. Add pasta and stir. Cook 6 minutes or until al dente. Using a slotted spoon, remove pasta from water and add directly to capon ragù.

8. Cook until pasta sauce begins to thicken a bit and coats the back of a spoon. Turn off heat and add butter, Urfa biber, and cheese and toss.

9. To serve, divide pasta among bowls. Add a spoon of whipped ricotta and a pinch of Urfa biber to each.

LELA'S BISCOTTI
Yields: 40 biscotti

2 cups sugar
Zest of 3 lemons
2¾ cups all-purpose flour
¼ cup whole wheat flour
1 heaping tablespoon baking powder
4 large eggs
3 cups sliced raw almonds

1. Preheat oven to 350°F.

2. Combine sugar and lemon zest in a large mixing bowl. Blend with your fingers to evenly incorporate. Add all-purpose flour, whole wheat flour, and baking powder on top and use a fork to blend all together. Make a well in the center and crack eggs into it. Use your hands to mix all together; knead until it forms a dough.

3. Line two baking sheets with parchment paper. Split dough evenly into two pieces; place one on each sheet. Use your fists to spread dough out to edges of baking sheet. Cover dough with almonds and press gently into dough. Repeat with the other piece of dough and the remaining almonds. Bake for 15 minutes until golden.

4. Remove from oven and slide dough onto the counter (still on parchment paper). Allow to cool for 20 to 30 minutes. When cool, peel off parchment paper and cut diagonal strips about 3/8 inch thick. Lay strips back onto baking sheet (parchment not necessary) with cut side facing up. Bake 12 to 15 minutes more until golden.

5. Serve biscotti with vanilla ice cream, garnished with edible gold dust (see Resources).

OPPOSITE: *Checking in with Akhtar Nawab, the chef for the evening and giving him a heads up on the expected dining time kept things running smoothly and seamlessly.* BELOW: *Lela's homemade biscotti was served alongside quenelles of vanilla ice cream covered in edible gold dust. An easy way to evenly dust the gold powder is to place the powder on a spoon and, while holding it over the bowl, gently blow.*

A COCKTAIL PARTY

Serves 8

ELDERBERRY FLOWER AND LEMONADE
CHAMPAGNE COCKTAIL**

SWEET POTATO BLINIS WITH SALMON,
CRÈME FRAÎCHE, AND DILL **

OPEN-FACED CROQUE MONSIEUR WITH RICOTTA **

ROASTED FINGERLING POTATOES WITH
CAVIAR AND BRANDADE**

TROUT TARTARE **

GALETTE WITH ONION SOUBISE, BENTON'S
COUNTRY HAM, AND SWISS CHEESE **

FRESH STRAWBERRIES WITH POWDERED SUGAR

VICTORIAN ICED SORBETS

CANAPÉS AND CROQUET

Inspired by one of my favorite books, F. Scott Fitzgerald's *The Great Gatsby*, which was first published about the same time that my house was built, I hosted an elegant lawn party in my backyard. I wanted guests to feel as if they had been transported to another era.

Invitations asked for "garden party-chic" attire, and the lower terrace of the formal lawn was soon a sea of filmy, romantic sundresses reminiscent of those Daisy Buchanan might have worn. Even the gentlemen, normally reluctant to dress up, got into the spirit with pastel and seersucker suits accented by bowties and bucks. Serving staff bearing brass-handled wicker serving trays greeted guests upon arrival with the drink of the afternoon, a refreshing cocktail of St.-Germain elderberry liqueur and lemonade. A small bar set up where guests arrived was covered in an antique linen tablecloth. To hide a huge hole in the old cloth that had been handed down through the generations (and all the

more treasured), an open wicker picnic hamper bursting with Boston ferns and a large glass hurricane vase filled with tall cheese straws served as both decoration and disguise. Sentiment always trumps perfection: If something I love doesn't fit just right or has a few spots from wear and tear, I still try to figure out a way to use it because it means more to me to have something very personal than very perfect. (Using what you have and having what you use is a great way to approach life in general!) Pink roses loosely arranged in a large glass goblet-style vase sat on the other side of the bar, creating an immediate welcome for a romantic sunset event. My three always helpful children (especially when their allowance is part of the deal) had spent their Saturday afternoon de-thorning buckets of roses in the shade of the loggia. A second, twelve-foot-long main bar at the end of the formal lawn, covered in loosely woven ivory linen and topped with a crisply ironed white vintage Army Navy tablecloth that I had purchased at the renowned Scott Antique Market, which is hailed as one of the treasures of the South, beckoned guests to head to the main lawn. Lush masses of spring roses in a single, overscale ivory-painted urn, flickering hurricane lamps, vintage silver cocktail shakers, and polished nickel-plated tubs filled with wine and Champagne created just the right note of Gatsby swell-egance. For larger events I like to have multiple bars in order to prevent guests from having to wait long to get a drink, but I always try to make one bar, where I really want people to congregate, the most attractive. Getting a crowd to move is a difficult task, and in large parties people always want to be where the action is.

A croquet instructor dressed all in white delighted guests with lessons on how to play American six-

PREVIOUS PAGE: *Mounds of pink garden roses in a painted lead urn created a stunning visual for the bar; elegant silver-plated tubs held Champagne.* ABOVE AND OPPOSITE: *It is always more exciting at a party to have your guests "travel." Everyone arrived at the front door, passed through the roses that were in full bloom in the side garden, and then sauntered onto the upper terrace, where the party was in full swing. That adventurous arrival, and the cold cocktail served in a tall, old-fashioned glass, put everyone in a festive mood.*

wicket croquet, a lawn sport tracing its roots to Victorian England. Entertaining and engaging, it kept both the people participating and those just observing equally happy. Waiters, attired in snappy white Nehru-collared jackets, passed out hors d'oeuvres on silver trays with intricately embroidered ivory and white monogrammed cocktail napkins with hand-crocheted scalloped edging.

Refreshing summer strawberries piled high in a silver-plated basket and a dipping bowl with powdered sugar, one of my favorite party treats to serve because it is both elegant and easy, was passed for guests to enjoy during dessert. Tiny fruit-shaped sorbets, inspired by iced confections that had once been the rage at the turn of the century and which I passed out to my delighted guests with a pair of silver tongs, added a culminating note of surprise and vintage charm to this spring soirée.

ELDERBERRY FLOWER AND LEMONADE CHAMPAGNE COCKTAIL

Lemonade (see recipe below)
1 bottle Champagne, chilled
8 ounces St.-Germain liqueur, chilled
8 highball glasses filled with crushed ice
8 thin lemon slices (for garnish)

LEMONADE
Yields: 8 Servings
2 cups freshly squeezed lemon juice (8 to 10 lemons)
2 cups sugar
2 cups water
4 cups cold water (to dilute)

1. Combine water and sugar in a saucepan and bring to a boil, stirring constantly, until sugar dissolves and the liquid becomes clear; reduce heat and simmer, stirring continually, 5 to 10 minutes.

2. Remove from heat and let cool to room temperature. Transfer syrup to a container and add lemon juice and cold water, tasting to get the perfect tart/sweet ratio: if you like it more tart, add more straight lemon juice; if you like it sweeter, add less. Store in an airtight container in the refrigerator for up to 2 weeks.

3. To serve, fill a highball glass to the top with crushed ice, then fill about two thirds full with lemonade. Top with 2 ounces Champagne and add 1 ounce St. Germain liqueur (liqueur is heavier than other liquids, so it should be added last)—do not stir. Serve with a straw and garnish with a thin slice of lemon.

3. Mix milk and egg together in a bowl; add to sweet potato puree and mix to combine.

4. Blend flour, baking powder, salt, and cayenne together in a bowl; fold into the sweet potato puree.

5. Place a baking sheet in the oven and preheat to 250°F. Melt a little bit of the remaining butter in a nonstick skillet over medium heat. Once it's hot, using a tablespoon, drop a dollop of the sweet potato batter into the skillet. Let cook 1 minute, then flip and cook until golden and crisp, about 1 minute more. Transfer blinis to the baking sheet in the oven. Continue with remaining sweet potato batter, using more butter as needed.

6. To serve, arrange blinis on a plate and garnish each with a slice of cured salmon, a dollop of crème fraîche, and a little sprig of dill.

OPEN-FACED CROQUE MONSIEUR WITH RICOTTA
Yields: 30 sandwiches

½ loaf sourdough bread, sliced (about 15 slices)
12 ounces Swiss cheese, thinly sliced
1 tablespoon unsalted butter, plus
  2 tablespoons butter for sautéing.
1 pint ricotta cheese
Sea salt and freshly ground black pepper
⅓ pound country ham, thinly sliced

1. Preheat oven to 350°F.

2. Cut crusts off bread slices and cut slices into 4 triangles. Cut cheese slices into triangles that are the same size as the pieces of bread.

3. Melt 1 tablespoon butter in a sauté pan over medium heat. Place ricotta in a mixing bowl; season with salt and pepper to taste. Drizzle melted butter into ricotta and stir.

4. Melt remaining 2 tablespoons butter in the sauté pan and add bread in batches. Toast bread on both sides.

5. Assemble sandwiches by placing toast on a baking sheet; put a piece of Swiss cheese on top of each one, followed by a spoonful of ricotta and then a slice of ham. Bake until cheese is melted, about 4 minutes. Serve immediately.

SWEET POTATO BLINIS WITH SALMON, CRÈME FRAÎCHE, AND DILL
Yields: 30 hors d'oeuvres

1 sweet potato, peeled
1 tablespoon honey
2 tablespoons soft unsalted butter,
  plus 3 tablespoons butter for sautéing
½ cup milk
1 large egg
¾ cup all-purpose flour
½ tablespoon baking powder
½ teaspoon sea salt
¼ teaspoon cayenne pepper
4 ounces cured salmon
¼ cup crème fraîche (for garnish)
4 dill sprigs (for garnish)

1. Preheat oven to 375°F.

2. Wash sweet potato and poke holes all over with a fork. Wrap in foil and bake until tender when pierced with a fork, about 45 minutes. Let cool, then push through a food mill or a tamis. Add honey and 2 tablespoons butter and mix until smooth.

ROASTED FINGERLING POTATOES WITH CAVIAR AND BRANDADE
Yields: 30 hors d'oeuvres

If you are pressed for time, use fresh cod, but make sure to season with enough salt. Serve any leftover brandade baked in a gratin dish with a simple green salad and toast points.

Roasted Fingerling Potatoes (see recipe below)
Brandade (see recipe below)
1 (1-ounce) tin of Osetra caviar

To serve, cut Roasted Fingerling Potatoes down the middle lengthwise and arrange on a serving platter. Place brandade in a piping bag and pipe filling into potato halves. Finish each with a small dollop of caviar on top.

BRANDADE
4 ounces salt cod
1 pound Yukon Gold potatoes
  (they do not need to be fingerlings)
1 pint heavy cream, plus up to 1 pint heavy
  cream for adding to puree
3 cloves garlic
⅓ cup olive oil
⅓ cup unsalted butter
Sea salt and freshly ground black pepper

1. Soak salt cod in fresh, cold water and refrigerate for 24 hours. Change water and soak again for 24 more hours. On the third day, prepare the brandade.

2. Cut potatoes into cubes; dice salt cod and place with the potatoes in a nonreactive pot. Cover with 1 pint cream and simmer until potatoes are tender.

3. Combine garlic and oil in a pan over medium-low heat until garlic is just golden and fragrant.

4. Drain potatoes and cod, discarding the liquid. Puree potatoes and cod in a food processor; add butter and garlic oil mixture, then add cream until mixture is smooth and spreadable. Season with salt and pepper to taste and chill.

ROASTED FINGERLING POTATOES
30 small Yukon Gold fingerling potatoes
¼ cup olive oil
1 teaspoon sea salt
2 pinches freshly ground black pepper

1. Preheat oven to 375°F.

2. Toss potatoes with oil, salt, and pepper. Place on a parchment-lined baking sheet and roast about 25 minutes, or until tender when pierced with a fork. Let cool.

TROUT TARTARE
Yields: 30 hors d'oeuvres

½ tablespoon lemon juice
¼ teaspoon Dijon mustard
1 tablespoon olive oil
1½ tablespoons clabbered (clotted) cream or crème fraîche
¼ pound cured trout, diced
Zest of 1 lemon
¼ tablespoon sweet-and-sour mustard seeds
¼ teaspoon freshly ground black pepper
½ teaspoon minced parsley

FOR GARNISH
25 benne wafers (see Resources)
25 grapefruit segments
25 pieces trout roe
25 pieces chive blossom

1. Whisk lemon juice and mustard together in a small bowl; slowly whisk in oil until blended. Gently fold in cream.

2. In a medium-size bowl, mix trout with lemon zest, mustard seeds, pepper, and parsley. Stir in lemon-mustard sauce and adjust seasoning to taste.

3. To serve, spoon a dollop onto each of the benne wafers and garnish each with a grapefruit segment, trout roe, and chive blossom.

GALETTE WITH ONION SOUBISE, BENTON'S COUNTRY HAM, AND SWISS CHEESE

Yields: 18 to 20 galettes

6 tablespoons unsalted butter
Crêpe Batter (see recipe below)
20 thin slices Benton's country ham (see Resources)
  or Black Forest ham
20 slices Swiss cheese
Onion Soubise (see recipe below)

1. Heat a nonstick crêpe pan and melt 1 teaspoon butter.

2. Pour ¼ cup crêpe batter into pan, cook 15 seconds then flip. Add ham, cheese, and soubise and cook 25 more seconds. Fold like an omelette, and serve immediately. Repeat to make more crêpes.

CRÊPE BATTER
1 ½ tablespoons unsalted butter
1 cup milk
½ tablespoon sugar
¼ teaspoon salt
¼ cup buckwheat flour
⅓ cup all-purpose flour
2 large eggs

1. Melt butter in a saucepan over medium heat.

2. Combine milk, sugar, and salt in a large bowl. Whisk in flours, then beat in eggs. Whisk in melted butter until smooth. Store, covered, in the refrigerator until ready to use (up to 12 hours).

ONION SOUBISE
½ cup unsalted butter
2 ½ pounds onions, thinly sliced
¼ cup heavy cream
1 ½ cups Béchamel Sauce (see recipe above)
Sea salt and freshly ground black pepper

1. Melt butter in a large saucepan. Add onions and cook over medium-low heat, stirring often, until translucent. Add cream and Béchamel Sauce. Season with salt and pepper.

2. Store in the refrigerator until ready to use, 2 to 3 days.

BÉCHAMEL SAUCE
3 tablespoons unsalted butter
2 tablespoons all-purpose flour
2 cups whole milk
1 teaspoon salt
½ teaspoon freshly grated nutmeg

1. Melt butter in a medium-size saucepan over low heat. Whisk in flour until smooth, then cook, stirring frequently so mixture doesn't brown, about 10 minutes.

2. Heat milk in a separate saucepan until just below a boil. Add hot milk to flour mixture, 1 cup at a time, whisking until very smooth. Bring to a boil. Season with salt and nutmeg and chill until ready to use, up to 3 days.

The gift of hospitality is the personal touches from the host or hostess that make a guest feel truly welcome. I always try to pass something around myself, which gives me the opportunity to mingle and mix with my guests in a relaxed manner and ensures that I get the chance to visit with everyone. OPPOSITE PAGE: Tiny sorbets (purchased from a gourmet food purveyor) molded in the shape of fruits were made even more elegant by replacing their original plastic leaves with mint.

A SPRING DINNER

Serves 8

ROLLINS COLLINS **

PIMENTO CHEESE FRITTERS **

VIDALIA ONION–BREBIS TARTS WITH FRISÉE SALAD,
BREAD-AND-BUTTER PICKLES, AND CITRUS VINAIGRETTE**

HERB-CRUSTED WILD SALMON, MOREL MUSHROOMS,
WILD GREENS, AND RED WINE FUMET **

ENGLISH PEA RAVIOLI WITH PANCETTA,
SHAVED BABY CARROTS, CELERY, AND MANDARINS **

STRAWBERRY SORBET WITH CRUMBLED COCOA

BIRDS OF A FEATHER: A CELEBRATION FOR A FLOCK OF MY FAVORITE FRIENDS

Every year when spring arrives and awakens our spirit, it feels like an amazing time to celebrate life and friendship. Transforming the swath of green carpeting on the lawn into an elegant outdoor dining room with decorations inspired by my love of birds and all things chinoiserie was quite simple. The delicate pale pink blossoms of the surrounding cherry trees, soft chartreuse dogwood blooms, fuchsia azaleas, and hundreds of peonies at the peak of spring-color perfection provided a perfect backdrop. And not only did the weather cooperate, but as any girly girl will attest, knowing that I had the perfect whimsical, feathery dress for the occasion filled me with pure excitement.

When hosting, I like to create mystery by unveiling each stage of the evening like a play with different acts. Guest entered the party through a canopy of lush hemlock trees surrounded by a camellia hedge in full bloom and then gathered in front of a large outdoor aviary, where the bar was set up. Everyone was greeted with a cucumber-infused, garden-themed Rollins Collins cocktail, garnished with edible orchids and served with playful green-and-white-striped paper straws.

The grand reveal was when guests entered the dining area. The "oohs" and "ahhs" made me smile. Centerpieces of goldfish in fishbowls, a nod to my inner Auntie Mame, were set atop bright orange lacquered plant stands on tables covered in vibrantly colored Asian motif tablecloths with vivid turquoise backgrounds that matched the chair seats. Silver julep cups held bunches of peonies, and clear votives and David Hicks's geometric-patterned candles finished the look. I don't have enough of any one set of a china for a large gathering, so I mixed several patterns in similar colors, creating an informal look that was more collected than catered. Napkins with colorful, embroidered floral letter Rs, bamboo-handled flatware, amethyst-colored water glasses, and aqua-bordered tented name cards written in a beautiful calligraphic hand in yellow ink tied the look together. Turquoise birdcages, suspended from gingham ribbon from the surrounding trees, complemented the night's enchanted garden theme. As the sky grew darker, a procession of

PREVIOUS PAGE: *A colorful place setting on a whimsically themed table cloth set the mood for fun.* THIS PAGE: *Colorful paper lanterns were strung across the koi pond from my closet window and anchored on the fence to create a festive area for dancing after dinner.*

servers brought out trays of additional prelit votives and added them to the tables. Adjusting the lighting created a gentle transition and boosted the magical ambiance, and, most important, guests could see their food.

The James Beard–nominated chef Linton Hopkins, from two of my favorite Atlanta restaurants, Restaurant Eugene and Holeman & Finch, created a sublime, springlike farm-to-table dinner. Fresh seasonal ingredients dictated the menu. We served Copper River salmon, only available a few weeks each spring, and English pea *agnolotti*. Tiny servings of strawberry sorbet, dusted with cacao, were the ideal finish before everyone hit the "Club Koi Disco." Bright, colorful paper lanterns were strung across the patio and over the koi pond for the post-dinner celebration. Ladies kicked off their Louboutins for some late-night dancing. Having a little personal disco gave us grownups, who otherwise might consider ourselves far too mature, a chance to indulge in a bit of youthful folly. Dancing makes people hungry, so a midnight snack of sliders and fries was served on silver trays, along with cake adorned with marzipan koi fish, lit with sparklers. What's one more indulgence to cap off a decadent night?

Celebratory libations were poured all night from a bar, which was appropriately draped in fabric with white koi swimming across a fuchsia background. Mixed hydrangeas in mirrored-glass fishbowls added a little more disco sparkle as the lantern's light danced on their surfaces, and decadent beds of hydrangeas were reflected in the koi pond, creating a backdrop bursting with shades of blue.

ROLLINS COLLINS

Limeade (see recipe below)
16 ounces Hendrick's Gin
Thinly sliced cucumber rounds
Edible micro orchids (see Resources)
Sparkling water
8 highboy glasses filled with crushed ice

LIMEADE
Yields: 8 servings
2 cups sugar
2 cups freshly squeezed lime juice (8 to 10 limes)

1. Combine 2 cups water and sugar in a saucepan and bring to a boil, stirring constantly, until sugar dissolves and liquid becomes clear; reduce heat and simmer, stirring continually, 5 to 10 minutes.

2. Remove from heat and let cool to room temperature. Transfer the syrup to a container and add lime juice and 4 cups cold water, tasting to get the perfect tart/sweet ratio:

if you like it more tart, add more straight lime juice; if you like it sweeter, add less. Store in an airtight container in the refrigerator for up to 2 weeks.

3. To prepare for serving, in a large pitcher, mix the limeade and Hendrick's Gin. Add sliced cucumber rounds.

4. To serve individual drinks, fill a highboy glass with crushed ice then the limeaid-gin mixture. Garnish with edible micro orchids (which add a slight cucumber taste) and top with a splash of sparkling water and a straw.

As with any party, sometimes there are a few mishaps that test a hostess's calm. While setting up for the party I noticed all of the birds had escaped their antique wicker bird cage—catching them required patience and agility! A good sense of humor is imperative to anyone who entertains often, and sometimes the calamity makes for great dinner conversation.

may 6th, 2011

‡

english pea agnolotti
house cured country ham
ed baby carrot & preserved satsuma

‡‡

lalia onion brebis cheese tart
frisee salad,
bread & butter pickles

‡‡‡

crusted wild king salmon
norel mushrooms,
red wine fumet

‡‡‡‡

wberry sorbet
idge strawberries

PREVIOUS PAGES: *The chinoiserie theme was carried throughout the party. Bright tablecloths created a dramatic punch of color on the grass lawn. A tiered cake with marzipan koi was a playful end-of-night celebration when brought out lit with sparklers! Goldfish bowls on lacquered Asian plant stands held river rocks and goldfish, adding a fanciful flare to the center of the tables.* ABOVE: *For a napkin that is as easy as it is pretty: Fold a napkin in half and then in half again face up, then flip down the top corner and turn over, folding both pointed sides together. Opposite: Names written on Post-It strips and placed on a diagram of the tables is a simple but tried-and-true method for seating charts. I recommend finalizing the seating the day of the party, instead of too far in advance, because there are always last-minute changes! Since I am always running late after setting up for a party, handing over a seating chart and the positioning of the place cards is a task I can always delegate—often to one of my children!*

Tommy Holder
Wayne Rollins
Kelly
Beth Holder
Hulse
Charles
Deborah Kelly
Mark
Ashley
Michael
Doug
Neil Johns
Lovette

PIMENTO CHEESE FRITTERS
Yields: 16 fritters

1 cup grated aged white sharp cheddar cheese
1 cup grated aged yellow extra-sharp cheddar cheese
4 tablespoons softened cream cheese
¼ cup mayonnaise, preferably homemade (or a store-bought brand that doesn't use sugar as an ingredient)
A couple shakes of Tabasco sauce
1 red bell pepper, charred over fire, peeled and diced
Salt and freshly ground black pepper
1 cup all-purpose flour
4 large eggs, lightly beaten
2 cups panko bread crumbs
Peanut oil, for frying
Spicy pepper jelly, thinned with a bit of warm water

1. Combine cheeses, mayonnaise, Tabasco, and red pepper in the bowl of a stand mixer with paddle attachment; blend on high for 30 seconds. Add salt and pepper to taste. This can be stored in the refrigerator in an airtight container for up to 2 days.

2. To prepare fritters, roll pimento cheese into 16 balls and refrigerate, uncovered, at least 30 minutes or covered, up to 24 hours.

3. Roll cheese balls in flour, then eggs, then panko. It is very important to cover the cheese balls completely in breading or they will disintegrate in the fryer. You may have to run the fritters through the bread-egg-panko steps twice.

4. Heat oil to 350°F. Fry fritters until just golden brown.

5. Serve fritters with a small dollop of the pepper jelly on top.

VIDALIA ONION–BREBIS TARTS WITH FRISÉE SALAD, BREAD-AND-BUTTER PICKLES, AND CITRUS VINAIGRETTE
Yields: 8 tarts

Tart dough (see recipe below)
4 tablespoons unsalted butter
2 cups minced Vidalia onions (about 2 onions)
2 large egg yolks
1 cup heavy cream
1 teaspoon salt
½ teaspoon freshly ground black pepper
4 tablespoons fresh brebis cheese (can substitute fresh goat cheese, Brie, or grated Parmigiano-Reggiano)

8 ounces frisée
¼ cup minced bread-and-butter pickles
Citrus Vinaigrette (see recipe below)

1. Preheat oven to 350°F.

2. Roll out dough to ⅛ inch thick. Let rest 30 minutes. Cut dough into circles to fit 8 tart molds, then fit gently into molds. Place wax paper into tart shells and fill with dried beans or pie weights. Bake tart shells until light golden brown, about 10 minutes. Remove shells from mold, let cool, and reserve.

2. Heat butter in a large pan over high heat. Add onions, stir; reduce heat to low, and cook, stirring occasionally, 1 hour or until onions are golden and caramelized. Reserve.

3. Whisk egg yolks and cream together; add salt and pepper.

4. Preheat the oven to 325°F. In each tart shell spread a layer of cooked onions and crumble 1 tablespoon cheese on top, then fill to the top with the egg-cream mixture. Place on a rimmed baking sheet and bake 10 minutes or until custard is set. Remove from oven.

5. Toss frisée with pickles and Citrus Vinaigrette. Season with salt and pepper to taste.

6. To serve, place each tart in the center of a plate and top with the dressed frisée.

TART DOUGH
2 cups all-purpose flour
½ teaspoon sea salt
½ teaspoon sugar
¾ cup unsalted butter, cut into ½-inch cubes
6 to 7 tablespoons ice water

1. In a bowl, whisk together flour, salt, and sugar. Using a pastry blender or two knives, cut in butter until pea-size crumbs form. Add water 1 tablespoon at a time and mix with your hands, adding more water as needed until the dough comes together. The dough should be moist but not sticky.

2. Turn dough out onto a lightly floured surface; divide into two balls and shape each into a 5-inch disk. Wrap in plastic and refrigerate for at least 1 hour.

CITRUS VINAIGRETTE

Zest of 1 orange
½ cup freshly squeezed orange juice (about 1 orange)
½ cup freshly squeezed grapefruit juice (about 1 grapefruit)
2 tablespoons sugar
2 teaspoons Dijon mustard
½ cup freshly squeezed lemon juice (about 2 lemons)
Sea salt and freshly ground black pepper
6 tablespoons peanut oil
Zest of 1 lemon
1 tablespoon minced fresh parsley

1. Put orange zest in a small saucepan with orange and grapefruit juices. Add sugar and simmer over low heat until reduced by two thirds. It should be nice and thick. Reserve at room temperature.

2. Whisk together mustard and lemon juice, then salt and pepper to taste in a medium-size bowl. Gradually whisk in oil, and the reserved orange-sugar syrup. Just before serving, stir in lemon zest and parsley.

HERB-CRUSTED WILD SALMON, MOREL MUSHROOMS, WILD GREENS, AND RED WINE FUMET

2 tablespoons unsalted butter
2 shallots, minced
1 pound morel mushrooms, cleaned
8 tablespoons veal jus (see Resources)
8 (6-ounce) skinless salmon fillets
Sea salt and freshly ground black pepper
8 squares Herb Crust (see recipe below)
2 cups baby greens such as dandelions, beet greens, purslane, or mâche

1. Preheat oven to 325°F.

2. Heat butter in medium-size pan until foamy. Add shallots and cook 2 minutes. Add morels and sauté 3 minutes. Reserve (can be stored in freezer up to 2 months).

3. Heat veal jus in a small saucepan over medium heat. Keep warm.

4. Season salmon with salt and pepper to taste. Top each with the herb crust and bake until fish is firm and flakes lightly and crust begins to lightly brown, 10 to 12 minutes.

5. To serve, place morels in the center of each plate. Place the salmon on top of the morels and garnish with greens. Spoon veal jus over the greens and onto the plate. Serve immediately.

HERB CRUST

¾ cup unsalted butter, softened
¾ cup combination minced fresh tarragon, parsley, and chives
1 cup fresh brioche bread crumbs (see recipe below)
Zest of 1 lemon
¼ teaspoon kosher salt
3 tablespoons freshly squeezed lemon juice (about 1 lemon)

1. Pulse butter with herbs in a food processor; slowly add bread crumbs, lemon zest, salt, and lemon juice until a soft ball of butter is formed.

2. Place on parchment paper, cover with another sheet of parchment, and roll flat with a rolling pin until the herbed butter is ⅛ inch thick.

3. Place in freezer until set, about 2 hours. Cut into squares the size of the fish portions and reserve.

1 loaf fresh brioche

1. Cube bread and bake in 200°F oven 30 minutes or until crisp and brown. Let cool.

2. Grind cubes in food processor. Store in airtight container up to 24 hours.

ENGLISH PEA RAVIOLI WITH PANCETTA, SHAVED BABY CARROTS, CELERY, AND MANDARINS

8 ounces Fresh Pasta Dough (see recipe below)
Semolina flour
English Pea Filling (see recipe below)
Salt
4 tablespoons unsalted butter
8 baked ⅛-inch-thick pancetta slices
8 baby carrots, peeled and shaved thin with a peeler
8 mandarin orange segments, pith removed
 and cut into thirds
16 celery leaves

1. Knead pasta dough a few times on a semolina-floured cutting board. Divide the dough into 3 equal-size pieces. Wrap two of the pieces in plastic wrap and set aside.

2. Roll out the remaining dough with a pasta machine set to its second-thinnest setting. Trim the edges so that they are straight.

3. Brush the bottom half of the pasta sheet with a little water.

4. Using a tablespoon, scoop up equal-size spoonfuls of pea filling and place along the bottom half of the pasta sheet, leaving a 1½-inch border of dough all around. Pull the top edge of the pasta up and over the filling. The dough should form one large pocket over the dollops of filling.

5. Seal the ravioli by gently and carefully molding the pasta over the filling and pressing lightly with your index finger to seal the edge of the dough to the pasta sheet. Don't drag your finger along the dough to seal, or you risk ripping the dough. When it is sealed, there should be about ½ inch of excess dough visible along the bottom of the mounds of filling, where you had sealed it. Be certain that you press out any pockets of air.

6. Run a sharp knife or crimped pastry wheel along the bottom edge of the folded-over dough, separating the strip of filled pockets from the remainder of the pasta sheet. Don't cut too close to the filling or you risk breaking the seal. Separate the individual ravioli by cutting in the center of each pinched area, rolling the pastry wheel away from you.

7. Dust a baking sheet with a thin layer of semolina, which will help prevent sticking. Place the ravioli on the baking sheet. Repeat with remaining pieces of dough (any excess dough may be refrigerated up to 3 days).

8. Boil fresh pasta in heavily salted water for 5 minutes. Drain and toss with butter to glaze.

9. To serve, place ravioli in bowl. Top with pancetta slices, carrots, orange pieces, and celery leaves.

FRESH PASTA DOUGH
Yields: About 1 pound
It's best to use a kitchen scale for the egg yolks and milk in this recipe since the size of egg yolks varies greatly.
3½ cups "00" farina flour or all-purpose flour
7 ounces egg yolks
2½ ounces whole milk
1½ tablespoons olive oil
Semolina flour (for dusting)

1. Combine flour, egg yolks, milk, and oil together in a bowl.

2. Knead dough on a lightly floured surface until smooth and elastic, about 20 minutes; let it rest 30 minutes.

ENGLISH PEA FILLING
1 cup shelled English peas
Sea salt
¼ cup bread crumbs
1 tablespoon unsalted butter
1 teaspoon freshly squeezed lemon juice (about ½ lemon)
¼ cup grated Parmigiano-Reggiano cheese

1. Cook peas in a pot of boiling, salted water until tender, about 2 minutes.

2. Rinse peas in ice-cold water, drain, and puree with bread crumbs, butter, lemon juice, cheese, and ¼ teaspoon salt until smooth. Reserve.

A SPRINGTIME BRUNCH

Serves 8

RUBY-RED GRAPEFRUIT AND MINT "MOM"OSAS **

HOMEMADE YOGURT AND GRANOLA **

FARMERS' MARKET FRITTATA **

BUTTERMILK BISCUITS AND JAMS

CANDIED BACON

FARRO GRITS **

LEMON RICOTTA PANCAKES WITH
LEMON CURD AND BLUEBERRIES **

ASSORTMENT OF HOLEMAN & FINCH BREADS
AND PASTRIES FROM FARMERS' MARKET

MOTHER'S DAY IN THE GARDEN

Every year I joke with my friends that the perfect Mother's Day would begin with a relaxing brunch under cloudless skies followed by a carefree afternoon with family and friends. Deciding that there was no time like the present, I invited all the special women in my life—four generations of my family, along with my closest girlfriends and their families—to a Sunday springtime brunch buffet on my rose-lined terrace. An antique folding tray table set up in the curtain-lined loggia held all the necessities for guests to serve themselves cocktails as needed and made for a relaxed, lazy Sunday. "Mom"osas, made with freshly squeezed grapefruit juice and Champagne accompanied by a sprig of fresh mint plucked from my herb garden, were the perfect breakfast beverage for the adults.

The two round tables on my terrace overlooking a pink rose garden were covered in pink-and-white-striped tablecloths that fell to the floor, with smaller, square, hand-embroidered floral overlays from Valombreuse layered over the cloths, making the tables look like a festive garden-party dress. Small terra-cotta pots planted with miniature pink roses and silver julep cups filled with bunches of radishes from my garden surrounded centerpieces of large white porcelain cachepots mounded with tightly packed peonies in shades of pink. Pickard china plates in the Elsie trellis pattern and bee-embossed glasses from La Rochere added a playful touch to complete the day's garden theme.

Everyone had their pick of treats from the buffet tables: Farmers' Market Frittatas; thick-cut, uncured bacon fried to crisp perfection and drizzled with maple syrup and brown sugar before being slowly roasted; Farro Grits; Homemade Yogurt sprinkled with freshly made granola and served in delicate white bone china tea cups; and Lemon Ricotta Pancakes topped with lemon curd and freshly picked blueberries. A smaller table held wicker baskets of homemade breads from Holeman & Finch, an artisanal bakery that's a local favorite: cinnamon twists, bagels, blueberry muffins, croissants, *pain au chocolat*, and homemade biscuits. On the side were artisanal jams, fresh cream cheese, and flavored butter whipped with a little bit of Maldon sea salt and honey. The children ran for the platters heaped with skewers of fresh fruit, which, of course, did double duty as swords after the fruit was eaten.

After brunch the mothers spent the afternoon lounging on the terrace, talking and browsing through the stash of newspapers and magazines set out for them. Husbands played bocce on the lawn, while the children put their feet in the koi pond and held pickup soccer games on the formal lawn. Having the chance to just sit and enjoy a Sunday afternoon with those we love was the perfect Mother's Day gift for all of us.

PREVIOUS PAGE: *Table settings were created to echo the gardens filled with pink roses around the patio.* OPPOSITE: *A pile of hats set aside for friends to grab as they sat down kept the sun off of all the moms' pretty complexions. Thinking through the details of guests' comfort and trying to anticipate needs is a mark of a good host.*

2. Pour milk into a nonreactive saucepan and whisk in the mixture of milk powder and carrageenan.

3. Heat milk to 180°F, then let it cool to 116°F. Add yogurt or starter and mix well.

4. Keep tightly covered in a warm place, between 80°F and 120°F, for at least 4 hours but no more than 8 hours. Tartness will depend on how long you leave it; the longer it is set out at room temperature, the tarter it gets.

5. To strain yogurt, lay a clean cloth napkin or piece of cheesecloth inside of a mixing bowl. Pour the yogurt in the cloth, then take up the four corners and tie string or butcher's twine around them to seal up the top. Tie the butcher's twine around a bamboo skewer and place across the mouth of the bowl, letting the cloth "bag" hang suspended over the bowl to catch the liquid as it drains. Refrigerate. The yogurt will have a firm consistency in about 12 hours. Discard the liquid and put the yogurt in an airtight container and refrigerate until ready to use. Yogurt will last at least 2 weeks refrigerated.

GRANOLA

2 cups rolled oats
1/3 cup wheat germ
1/4 cup slivered almonds
1/4 cup pecans, coarsely chopped
1/4 cup walnuts, coarsely chopped
1/4 cup sunflower seeds
1/3 teaspoon salt
1/4 cup dark brown sugar
Dash of maple syrup
1/4 cup honey
1/4 cup grapeseed oil
1/4 tablespoon ground cinnamon
1/4 tablespoon vanilla extract
1/3 cup dried cherries
1/3 cup dried apples, chopped

1. Preheat oven to 225°F. Mix all ingredients together in a large bowl.

2. Spread on a Silpat or other silicone mat on a baking sheet and bake for 20 minutes, rotate, then bake another 20 minutes.

3. Let granola cool completely, then store in an airtight container up to 2 weeks. Serve with yogurt.

RUBY-RED GRAPEFRUIT AND MINT "MOM"OSAS

8 sprigs fresh mint (for muddling), plus 8 more for garnish
32 ounces ruby-red grapefruit juice
  (6 to 8 medium grapefruit)
1 bottle Champagne, chilled
8 mint julep cups, plus enough crushed ice to fill them

To make individual drinks, place a mint sprig in a mint julep cup and muddle to extract the mint's flavor. Fill the cup to the top with ice, then three quarters of the way full with fresh grapefruit juice and top with Champagne. Garnish with a fresh mint sprig.

HOMEMADE YOGURT AND GRANOLA

YOGURT

2½ tablespoons dry milk powder
1¾ teaspoons carrageenan (optional, for thicker yogurt)
1 quart whole milk
2 tablespoons yogurt with live cultures, or 1 packet
  starter culture

1. Mix milk powder and carrageenan (if using) in a medium-size bowl thoroughly to prevent clumping.

FARMERS' MARKET FRITTATA

3 slices bacon, cut crosswise into ¼-inch pieces
2 tablespoons unsalted butter
1 bunch green garlic (or 3 cloves garlic, thinly sliced)
1 bunch spinach, washed and stems removed
Sea salt and freshly ground pepper
1 dozen large eggs

1. Preheat oven to 375°F.

2. Put bacon and butter in a large ovenproof skillet over medium-high heat.

3. Cook, stirring occasionally, until bacon is crisp; add garlic and spinach. Cook until spinach is just wilted. Season with salt and pepper to taste. Make sure spinach mixture is evenly distributed on bottom of skillet.

4. Crack eggs into a blender and add 1 teaspoon salt and freshly ground pepper to taste. Blend until eggs are foamy, about 15 seconds.

5. Pour eggs onto spinach and cook over low heat just until the eggs on the side of the pan start set; place pan in the oven. Frittata will be done when a toothpick or skewer inserted into it comes out clean, about 15 minutes.

FARRO GRITS

1 pound farro
1½ cups heavy cream
¼ cup grated Parmigiano-Reggiano cheese
Sea salt and freshly ground pepper

1. In a medium-size pot, bring 3 quarts water to a boil and whisk in the farro. Reduce heat to medium low and cook about 20 minutes or until tender. Drain any excess water and return the farro to the pot. Add cream, reduce heat to low, and cook, stirring occasionally, until the farro is creamy, about 4 minutes.

2. Stir in cheese and season with salt and pepper to taste. Serve hot.

LEMON RICOTTA PANCAKES WITH LEMON CURD AND BLUEBERRIES

LEMON CURD

Yields: 2 cups
3 large egg yolks
½ cup sugar
4 to 5 tablespoons freshly squeezed lemon juice
  (about 2 lemons)
Zest of 24 lemons
4 tablespoons unsalted butter, diced

1. Put 2 cups water in a medium-size saucepan and bring to a simmer. Combine egg yolks and sugar in a medium-size metal mixing bowl and blend. Add lemon juice and zest. Place the mixing bowl with the yolks and sugar on top of the saucepan and whisk constantly until mixture thickens, 7 to 10 minutes. When the yolks lighten in color and coat the back of a spoon, remove the pan from heat and slowly add butter to the curd, whisking constantly.

2. When butter is melted, store curd in a container and place plastic wrap directly on the surface of the curd to prevent a skin from developing. Refrigerate until ready to use (up to 2 weeks in an airtight container).

LEMON RICOTTA PANCAKES

16 large eggs, yolks and whites separated
32 ounces ricotta
12 tablespoons sugar
2 cups all-purpose flour
Zest of 3 lemons
½ cup unsalted butter
Lemon Curd (recipe above)
2 pints blueberries

1. Combine egg yolks, ricotta, sugar, flour, and lemon zest in a medium-size mixing bowl.

2. In a separate mixing bowl, whip egg whites to stiff peaks.

3. Add a spoonful of the yolk mixture into the whipped whites and gently fold in. Add the egg whites to rest of yolk mixture and gently fold in, taking care not to overmix.

4. Heat a skillet over medium heat and add a small amount of butter. Ladle a spoonful of batter into the pan and cook until it begins to bubble and turn golden; flip and cook the other side until golden, 10 to 15 seconds. Serve immediately with Lemon Curd and blueberries.

AN AFTERNOON TEA

Serves 8

COMING UP ROSES **

GEORGIA TROUT MOUSSE PROFITEROLES **

RADISH, GOAT CHEESE, AND PRESERVED LEMON CANAPÉS **

STRAWBERRY GAZPACHO **

CUCUMBER AND YOGURT CANAPÉS **

WATERCRESS TEA SANDWICHES WITH
SHRIMP ON PUMPERNICKEL **

FLAVORED MARSHMALLOWS

MINI ICE CREAM CONES WITH STRAWBERRY ICE CREAM

COCONUT CAKE, PETIT FOURS,
STRAWBERRY CUPCAKES, AND ICED SUGAR COOKIES

SELECTION OF TEAS

SOMETHING BORROWED, SOMETHING PINK!

Best-selling author and dear friend Emily Giffin, hailed by *Vanity Fair* as a "modern-day Jane Austen," deserved a proper toast for the silver-screen premiere of her very first movie, *Something Borrowed*. Emily and I both agree that one of the best parts of a party is getting dressed for the party, so a small group of girlfriends came a little early for a rare treat—a girly primping session! Having a hair stylist and makeup artists on hand in my dressing room turned beauty parlor created a carefree afternoon for the small group sipping Champagne and savoring a light lunch of finger sandwiches while leisurely getting ready.

Later in the afternoon, the rest of the ladies arrived dressed in pink or white as the invitations instructed, for a full-tilt English tea worthy of any bridal celebration. In the center of

PREVIOUS PAGES: *A table covered in a wildly patterned print was a bright gathering spot for all the ladies. An arrangement of peonies, vivid pink hydrangeas, rosemary, and mint packed a visual punch on the bar.* ABOVE AND OPPOSITE: *Chantecaille makeup artists from Neiman Marcus, matching spa robes from Cosabella, and a basket piled high with pink Spanx and goody bags stuffed to the brim with treats to take home created an indulgent, pampered mood.*

the patio, a table covered in hot pink denim with a wildly printed floral fabric overlay created an ultra-femme bar. A bartender in a pink apron manned the bar set up with silver-plated ice coolers filled with bottles of rosé Champagne, pitchers of ice water with sliced strawberries and mint, and a tray of cocktails neatly lined up all at the ready to serve the ladies. Two round tables swathed in buoyant pink-and-white-striped fabric were piled high with light hors d'oeuvres and a mountain of sweets: fluffy coconut cake, mini strawberry cupcakes, scones, lemon cookies, pastel marshmallows, and strawberry gazpacho served in etched silver shot glasses. Since I wanted to enjoy my morning with Emily, the doyenne of the day, the sweets were ordered in advance and picked up the morning of the tea from a favorite bakery. Taking my cue from chic Parisiennes, I tend to seek out the very best treats I can purchase rather than making them myself so that I can enjoy the extra time primping for a party!

When entertaining I always aim for a few "Wow!" moments—in this case, Coming up Roses, a lovely libation served with rose petals over crushed ice and garnished with a cheerful green-and-white-striped straw. As the ladies lifted a glass of pink Champagne and made a toast to Emily, a group photo was taken of the guests standing in the center of the courtyard by a photographer perching on the ledge of a second-floor window. Like a scene from one of Emily's novels, at the magic hour, all the ladies departed the gathering and went to the theater to walk the pink carpet of the film's premiere—an experience made more poignant after a day spent reconnecting with our closest girlfriends. Truly a happy ending to a picture-perfect day!

ABOVE: *Ladies indulged in a delectable confection or two while enjoying a beautiful afternoon in the garden.* OPPOSITE: *Tea cups stacked a bit ramshackle and tins of Harney & Sons teas casually laid out for self-service on a table created a delightfully casual feeling for an otherwise proper tea.*

COMING UP ROSES

8 ounces Lime or Raspberry Simple Syrup
  (see recipe below)
16 ounces freshly squeezed lime juice
  (8 to 10 limes) *many grocery stores
  will squeeze upon request, which makes
  it much easier!
4 ounces rose syrup, plus a splash for each drink
16 ounces Bacardi Razz rum
Fresh, edible rose petals that have not been treated
  with pesticide (see Resources)
1 bottle Champagne, chilled
8 tall highboy glasses filled with crushed ice

LIME OR RASPBERRY SIMPLE SYRUP
1 cup sugar
Zest of 1 lime and/or ½ pint raspberries

1. Combine 1 cup water and sugar in a saucepan and bring
   to a boil, stirring constantly, until sugar dissolves and the
   liquid becomes clear; reduce heat and simmer, stirring
   continually, 5 to 10 minutes.

2. Remove from heat and add lime zest and/or raspberries. Let cool to room temperature, then strain the
   liquid through a fine-mesh sieve into a container,
   discarding the fruit. Store in an airtight container in the
   refrigerator up to 2 weeks.

3. To prepare for serving, in a large pitcher, combine simple
   syrup mixture, lime juice, rose syrup, and rum.

4. To serve individual drinks, muddle a few fresh rose petals with a splash of the rose syrup in the bottom of a tall
   highboy glass, then fill with crushed ice. Fill glass with
   the rum mixture about three quarters of the way and
   top with about 2 ounces Champagne. Add a splash of
   rose water and a small handful of rose petals to the glass
   and serve with a straw.

TROUT MOUSSE

4 ounces smoked trout
12 ounces cream cheese, softened
Sea salt and freshly ground black pepper
Capers (for garnish)

1. Pulse smoked trout in a food processor until chopped up.

2. Add cheese and blend until incorporated. Season
   with salt and pepper to taste.

3. To assemble, place Trout Mousse in a piping bag with a
   star tip or in a ziplock bag, cutting one corner off. Slice the
   tops off the profiteroles and pipe mousse into each.

4. Garnish each with a caper and serve.

RADISH, GOAT CHEESE, AND PRESERVED LEMON CANAPÉS
Yields: 30 canapés

½ cup sugar
½ cup sea salt, plus more to taste
Zest of 3 lemons, plus 1½ tablespoons lemon juice
  (about ½ lemon)
30 round radishes, preferably Easter Egg
8 ounces chèvre (soft goat cheese)
Freshly ground black pepper
¼ cup olive oil
Chive tips (for garnish)

1. Pour 1 cup water, sugar, and salt in a small saucepan
   over high heat and bring to a boil.

2. Zest lemons with a bartender's zester to make long
   strips with no pith. Pour the boiling water over the
   lemon strips in a heatproof container and cover;
   let steep at least 30 minutes.

3. Cut the tops and bottoms off the radishes so they sit
   evenly on a tray. Use a small melon baller to hollow
   out the inside of each radish.

4. Mix goat cheese in a bowl with salt, pepper, oil, and lemon
   juice. Place cheese mixture in a piping bag with a star tip. Pipe
   goat cheese into radishes.

5. To serve, garnish each with a chive tip and a ribbon
   of preserved lemon.

GEORGIA TROUT MOUSSE PROFITEROLES
Yields: 60 profiteroles

PÂTE À CHOUX FOR PROFITEROLES

⅔ cup unsalted butter
Pinch of sea salt
1 cup all-purpose flour
4 or 5 large eggs, lightly blended

1. Preheat oven to 425°F. Heat butter, 2 tablespoons water, and
   salt in a medium-size pot until the butter is melted. Add
   flour all at once, stirring with a wooden spoon; continue to
   cook, stirring constantly over low heat, until mixture forms
   a dough and pulls away from the sides of the pot.

2. Immediately place dough in the bowl of a stand mixer with
   a paddle attachment and mix on medium speed. Slowly
   incorporate eggs, one at a time, into the dough. Stop
   adding eggs when the mixture is soft enough to pipe but
   not runny.

3. Place dough in a piping bag with a plain tip and pipe onto
   a parchment-lined sheet pan, making 60 small puffs.
   Bake 10 minutes. Rotate pan and bake another 5 minutes.
   Reduce heat to 400°F and bake until golden brown.
   Remove from oven and let cool.

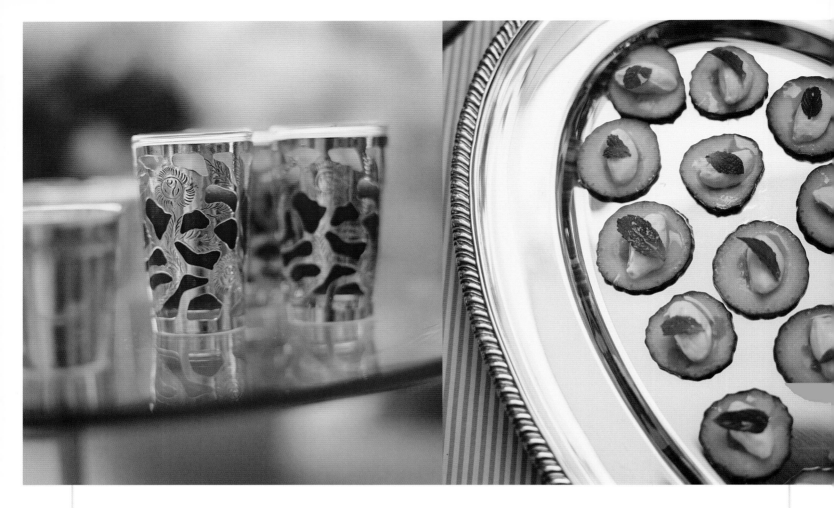

STRAWBERRY GAZPACHO

5 pints ripe strawberries
1 small cucumber
1 cup freshly squeezed orange juice (available in the
    produce area of most grocery stores or from 2 to 3 oranges)
1 cup toasted slivered almonds, plus more for garnish
⅓ cup extra-virgin olive oil, plus more for garnish
Aged balsamic vinegar (for garnish)

1. Rinse strawberries and cut off tops. Place strawberries,
   cucumber, orange juice, and almonds in a blender and
   puree in batches. Drizzle a couple tablespoons oil into each
   batch until the oil is all gone. Strain gazpacho through a
   fine-mesh strainer over a medium-size bowl, reserving the
   liquid and discarding the solids.

2. Divide soup evenly among 8 small cups; garnish with a
   drizzle of olive oil, slivered almonds, and a drop of aged
   balsamic vinegar. Serve immediately.

CUCUMBER AND YOGURT CANAPÉS
Yields: 40 canapés

1 quart thick plain yogurt
2 English cucumbers
3 tablespoons extra-virgin olive oil,
    plus 1 tablespoon for garnish
Sea salt and freshly ground black pepper
1 bunch fresh mint

1. Place a clean cloth napkin or cheesecloth in a colander.
   Pour yogurt into the cheesecloth and tie up the four
   corners with kitchen string. Place the colander in a larger
   bowl to catch liquid; refrigerate for 12 hours.

2. Slice cucumbers into ½-inch-thick rounds; set on paper
   towels to drain.

3. Put strained yogurt in a mixing bowl and add 3 tablespoons
   oil; season with salt and pepper to taste. Mix thoroughly.

4. To serve, arrange cucumber slices on a platter and spoon a
   dollop of yogurt on top of each. Drizzle with remaining oil
   and garnish each with a mint leaf.

WATERCRESS TEA SANDWICHES
WITH SHRIMP ON PUMPERNICKEL
Yields: 30 sandwiches

2 pounds fresh raw shrimp
2 tablespoons unsalted butter, plus more for toasting bread
1 carrot
1 onion, preferably Vidalia
1 bay leaf
Sea salt and freshly ground black pepper
1 bunch watercress
12 ounces cream cheese, softened
2 loaves sliced pumpernickel bread with the crusts removed

1. Peel and devein shrimp. Reserve shells.

2. Heat a medium-size saucepan over medium-high heat. Add 1 tablespoon butter to the pan. Add shrimp shells, carrot, and onion and cook until the shells turn dark pink. Add 2 quarts water and bay leaf and simmer 30 minutes.

3. Strain and return liquid to the pan, adding a couple pinches of salt, and return to a low simmer. Poach shrimp in the barely simmering liquid until opaque, about 3 minutes. Drain shrimp and spread on a plate or a baking sheet and let cool in the refrigerator. When cool, slice shrimp in half.

4. Wash and dry watercress and place in a food processor. Pulse for about 30 seconds; add cream cheese. Mix until incorporated, then season with salt and pepper to taste.

5. Cut pumpernickel slices into quarters or other bite-sized shapes (you can use a small biscuit cutter or a cookie cutter). Melt remaining 1 tablespoon butter in a sauté pan and add bread. Toast bread on both sides.

6. Spread a generous amount of watercress spread on a piece of toast and top with a second piece of toast. Put a small dollop of watercress spread on top, then cover with half a shrimp, cut side down. Repeat with the remaining ingredients. Serve immediately.

Tiny ice cream cones with miniature scoops of Bluebell's seasonal 'Strawberries and Cream' ice cream were served with pride by my adorable "Mini Me" hostess, Carlyle, to great satisfaction, judging by the ladies' "oohs" and "aahs." A tiny indulgence that felt almost guilt free!

A SUMMER DINNER
Serves 8

PROSECCO LIMONCELLO SPARKLERS **

ANTIPASTO

FARMERS' MARKET SALAD **

FRESH TOMATO SAUCE **

PIZZA DOUGH **

GEORGIA THREE-CHEESE PIZZA **

BACON, KALE, AND GOAT CHEESE PIZZA **

STRAWBERRY-BASIL ICE POPS WITH PROSECCO **

PEACH-MINT ICE POPS WITH PROSECCO **

PIZZA PARLOR AL FRESCO

As soon as I tasted the wood-fired-oven pizza from the Moto Bene truck at the St. Philips Farmers' Market, I could not contain my excitement. After my first piping-hot bite, I booked Dan Latham, formerly of Mario Batali's Babbo, and his crew for a pizza parlor–inspired dinner al fresco to welcome the summer for my dearest *amici!*

Invitations printed in dark green ink on craft paper were pasted inside small cardboard pizza boxes and mailed. Doing something out of the ordinary ensures that, from the moment an

invitation is opened, guests know they are in for a fun night! Next, it was all about creating an unpretentious atmosphere to match the laid-back menu. My favorite way to entertain outdoors is dining on one very long table because not only is it dramatic, it also keeps everyone connected—round table groupings sometimes split up a group, and it is tricky to get the seating right. To create a graphic punch on the green lawn and achieve a pizza-party feel, black-and-white gingham fabric, always chic, was made into tablecloths, placed end to end, and laid on top of a rustic burlap tablecloth recycled from a previous party. A fragrant mini herb garden featuring simple clay pots of basil, oregano, rosemary, parsley, and tomato plants tied with raffia to bamboo trellises served as table decoration and reinforced the summery *giardino* Italiano vibe. Instead of traditional place cards, tiny clay pots, each with a packet of herb seeds and a guest's name written on a wooden garden marker, were placed at the top of each place setting.

With the chefs' prep area set up at the end of the garden, the ingredients for pizzas were arranged into attractive displays featuring heaping bowls of tomatoes and cheese and canisters of flour. Menu cards bearing a boxwood emblem and printed on simple craft paper listed all the seasonal pizza ingredients and toppings so that guests could order individual custom pies. The pizzas were cooked

ABOVE: *Menu cards printed in green ink on craft paper tempted guests with what was to come, while clay pots served as place cards. Simple metal trash cans painted in black and cream stripes turned an object of necessity into a chic garden statement.* OPPOSITE PAGE: *Boxwood-patterned napkins emblazoned with a monogrammed R perfectly complemented the garden-themed Italian pottery dinnerware, which was festooned with boxwoods, knot gardens, and trellises. Forest-green bubble glass tumblers from Target set just the right tone of casual elegance when mixed with plain stemware.*

molto rapidly in the wood-burning oven and served on wooden pizza paddles that were passed down the table for congenial sharing.

Simple, inexpensive Italian table wines complemented the pizzas. Large maple-wood bowls of mixed greens from a local farm, dressed with balsamic vinaigrette, were added to the table just before everyone sat down. For a sophisticated twist on a childhood favorite, fruit and herb ice pops were dropped into a wineglass filled with Prosecco, which playfully combined dessert and drink for fun and function and added the perfect ending to the al fresco, on-the-cusp-of-summer fest.

PROSECCO LIMONCELLO SPARKLERS

4 lemons, cut into wedges
1 cup sugar
8 wide strips lemon zest made with a vegetable peeler
8 tablespoons limoncello
1 bottle Prosecco, chilled
8 tall glasses with enough ice cubes to fill them

Rub a lemon wedge along rim of each glass and dip rim in sugar. Place a strip of lemon zest in each glass and fill with ice. Add limoncello and top with Prosecco. Squeeze a bit of fresh lemon juice into each glass and serve immediately.

FRESH TOMATO SAUCE

1 (28-ounce) can San Marzano
  (whole, peeled, without basil) tomatoes
1½ tablespoons extra virgin olive oil
2 teaspoons salt

Mix all ingredients in a large container. Using an immersion blender, blend until tomatoes and oil are combined. If you do not have an immersion blender use a traditional blender or even a food mill. This sauce should be silky and thoroughly pureed, not chunky.

PIZZA DOUGH

4 cups "Caputo 00" pizzeria flour or all-purpose flour
4 teaspoons salt
½ tablespoon active dry yeast
1½ cups ice-cold water *
2 tablespoons extra virgin olive oil

1. Combine all dry ingredients together in the bowl of a stand mixer and add water and oil. Make sure not to pour the cold water directly onto the yeast. Using cold water stunts the growth of the yeast so the fermentation happens slowly, creating a more flavorful dough. Mix on the lowest speed for 3 minutes and then on the highest speed for 5 minutes. The mixing action creates friction and heats the dough, which activates the yeast. If you do not have a mixer, combine all the ingredients in a bowl and work them by hand until a loose dough ball forms. Turn dough out on a lightly floured surface and knead aggressively for 7 to 10 minutes, adding flour when dough seems too wet. Please note this dough by nature is wet and can be difficult to handle.

2. Cover dough and let rise for 45 minutes or until almost doubled in size. Punch down dough and form into a large ball, then cut into 4 equal pieces.

3. Form a dough ball by gently rolling one of the dough pieces in the palm of your hand. Be sure to stretch the top of the ball down and around the rest of the ball, until the outer layer wraps around the other side. Pinch the two ends together to make a smooth ball. Repeat with remaining 3 balls. Dust pizza balls with flour, and store under a damp towel, in a proofing tray, or on a sheet pan covered with plastic wrap. This will prevent the outside of the ball from drying out and creating a crust. The top of the pizza ball should be soft and supple.

4. Let pizza balls rest in a cool place for at least 1 hour before stretching. If you will not be using your pizza balls right away you can refrigerate up to 24 hours or freeze them in individual plastic freezer bags.

BACON, KALE, AND GOAT CHEESE PIZZA

1 fresh dough ball (see recipe, page 106)
¼ cup good-quality extra-virgin olive oil
1 cup wilted kale
¼ cup Sweet Water chèvre (or other fresh goat cheese)
½ cup cooked chopped bacon

1. Stretch dough to approximately 14 inches round and spread 2 tablespoons oil over dough. Evenly distribute kale, cheese, and bacon over pie. Be careful to nicely cover kale with cheese or it will burn and taste bitter.

2. Pull pizza onto a peel and cook in a wood fired oven or super-hot (500°F or hotter) conventional oven until nicely charred and cheese just starts to melt. Slice and serve.

HOME PIZZA-MAKING TIPS FROM DAN LATHAM

If you are like me and don't have an industrial range or a Big Green Egg at home, don't fret. My GE blasts away at 550°F, which is totally adequate to make great pizza at home. Just make sure you preheat for at least 30 minutes and don't disturb the oven. If you have a pizza stone, great, use it. If not, invert a half sheet pan for a similar effect. Just make sure in either case that you preheat the stone or pan adequately. On a side note, you will need a wooden peel to slide the pizza into the oven and metal peel or large spatula to remove it. I have used cardboard, sheet trays, you name it, but nothing beats a good peel.

Also be prepared for hot bubbly cheese to be on the bottom of your oven. It just happens—a lot.

Have an abundance of good ingredients on hand like extra-virgin olive oil, flour, canned tomatoes, and fresh mozzarella.

As well as the peels, make sure you have a good ladle or large spoon for applying the sauce. Finally, make sure you have a large cutting board or some place you can cut the pizza. Nothing is worse than bringing a pizza out of a very hot oven and having nowhere to go with it. Not that I would know anything about this . . .

GEORGIA THREE-CHEESE PIZZA

1 fresh dough ball (see recipe, page 106)
½ cup fresh tomato sauce
1 ounce Sweetgrass Dairy Green Hill cheese (or Camembert)
1 ounce Sweetgrass Dairy Tomme cheese (or Cantal or Comté)
1½ ounces Atlanta Fresh Mozzarella (or other fresh mozzarella)
6 basil leaves
1 to 2 tablespoons good-quality extra-virgin olive oil

1. Stretch dough to approximately 14 inches round and spread a thin layer of sauce over dough. Sprinkle evenly with cheeses and top with fresh basil. Drizzle with half the oil.

2. Pull pizza onto a peel and cook in a wood-fired oven or super-hot (500°F or hotter) conventional oven. Cook until dough is nice and charred and cheese is melted. Remove from oven and drizzle with remaining oil. Slice and serve.

THIS PAGE: *Wooden serving boards held grilled asparagus tossed lightly with lemon, olive oil, and shaved Parmesan, and a tray of antipasto assembled from salami, prosciutto, and Italian cheeses made for both and attractive and tasty display. Olive oil–brushed lightly grilled bread served alongside a platter of vine-ripe tomatoes, seasoned with sliced onion and a splash of balsamic vinegar, made for make-your-own bruschetta on the self-serve bar. A little nibble at the bar is a thoughtful touch when entertaining.* OPPOSITE: *Dan Latham working his magic.*

STRAWBERRY-BASIL ICE POPS WITH PROSECCO

¾ to 1 cup packed brown sugar
  (depending on sweetness of berries)
4 cups fresh ripe strawberries, stems removed
3 tablespoons fresh basil leaves
2 tablespoons freshly squeezed lemon juice
12 ice pop molds and sticks

1. Combine 2 cups water and brown sugar in a medium saucepan over high heat. Bring to a boil, reduce heat to medium, and cook until sugar dissolves into a simple syrup. Remove from heat and let cool.

2. In a blender, combine 2 cups strawberries with basil leaves and 1 tablespoon lemon juice; pulse until blended. Set aside. Repeat with remaining strawberries, basil, and lemon juice. Divide simple syrup evenly among batches.

3. Pour into ice pop molds and freeze at least 6 hours (ice pops will keep in freezer up to 2 weeks).

4. Place ice pop upside down in a wineglass and pour Prosecco over. Serve immediately.

PEACH-MINT ICE POPS WITH PROSECCO

6 ripe peaches, peeled, pitted, and sliced
3 tablespoons freshly squeezed lime juice
4 tablespoons finely chopped mint
½ to ¾ cup sugar
¼ teaspoon ground Vietnamese cinnamon (optional)

1. Place peaches, lime juice, 2 tablespoons mint, sugar, and cinnamon (if using) in a blender and blend to combine. Taste and add more lime juice or sugar. Stir in remaining mint.

2. Pour into ice pop molds and freeze at least 6 hours (ice pops will keep in freezer up to 2 weeks).

3. Place ice pop upside down in a wineglass and pour Prosecco over. Serve immediately.

FARMERS' MARKET SALAD

2 bags mixed baby greens
6 radishes, very thinly sliced
1 English cucumber, very thinly sliced
2 carrots, very thinly sliced or peeled with a vegetable peeler
1 pint grape tomatoes, sliced in half
1 cup crumbled feta cheese
Salad Dressing (see recipe below)

Toss all ingredients together in a bowl. Drizzle with dressing and toss to coat.

SALAD DRESSING

1 small can flat anchovies, drained and finely diced
3 to 4 cloves garlic, pressed in a garlic press
Juice of 2 lemons
2 tablespoons Dijon mustard
1 cup olive oil
Sea salt and freshly ground pepper to taste

Place all ingredients in a food processor and pulse to combine thoroughly or whisk by hand until emulsified.

A FRENCH PICNIC
Serves 8

SALAD OF MÂCHE, ARUGULA,
AND PINE NUTS WITH FRENCH VINAIGRETTE **

LEMON AND GARLIC GRILLED CHICKEN BREAST ON
BULGUR SALAD WITH FRESH HERBS **

ASSORTMENT OF SMALL SANDWICHES **

VANILLA RICE PUDDING WITH
CANDIED FRUIT AND APRICOT COMPOTE **

FRESH APRICOTS

AN AFTERNOON BY THE SEA

Throwing any party has its share of planning, preparation, and logistical challenges, but hosting one at a rented villa on the French Riviera the day after a surprise birthday party might just take the cake—and one with fifty candles! My good friend Ashley Dabbiere planned a surprise weekend for her husband Alan's fiftieth birthday in Villefranche-sur-Mer, and we threw a pool party and picnic the day after the surprise party to recap the fun from the night before.

Our vision was the relaxed, cosmopolitan feel of a European beach club—think Club 55 in Saint-Tropez meets the aristocratic elegance of a Slim Aarons–style pool party and picnic. Having such beautiful scenery meant only a little effort was needed to create a perfect party backdrop, and letting the environment dictate the mood of any party makes for much easier planning. A buffet table covered in tablecloths fashioned from Schumacher's Kerala indigo ikat held inexpensive bread baskets bought locally to serve as individual picnic baskets—as *très chic* as they were practical: economical, compact, and all-in-one dining with minimal cleanup required. Guests' faces actually

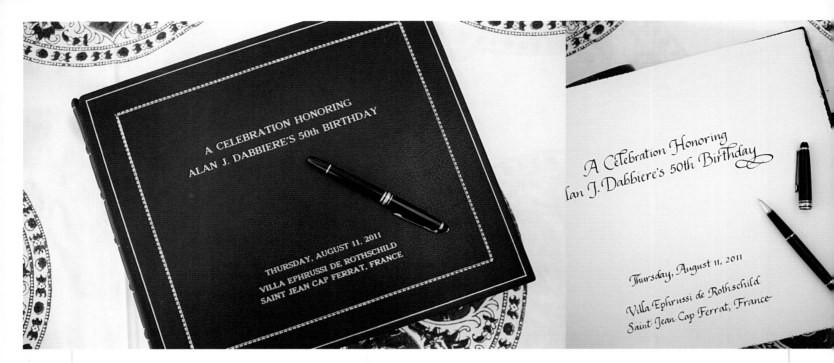

lit up with delight when they found a plate, napkin, silverware, and lunch all tucked inside. Bamboo-handled silverware procured in Paris from Philippe Chupin of Siècle were rolled up inside Les Indiennes napkins and tied tightly with raffia. Dishwasher-safe and eco-friendly Mottahedeh Turkish Garden tin plates brought with us from home created a breezy ambiance of Mediterranean chic.

For entertainment, the dapper sommelier Stéphane Bonnerot brought a case filled with tiny glass vials of different scents: flowers, herbs, and other vine-influenced aromas to refine our wine sensibilities. You often hear that a wine has a chalky taste or a floral undertone, so to have the ability to experience the scent and then taste the wine was an excellent way to educate the palate—not to mention a great icebreaker. Guests were also introduced to the art of *sabrage*, a French tradition dating back to Napoleon in which military cavaliers, to celebrate victory, sliced the tops of the Champagne bottles off using their sharp-edged sabers. (In victory one deserves it, in defeat one needs it!) I am normally gifted with nerves of steel, but having a crowd watch me wielding a giant sword and a heavier-than-you-would-expect Champagne bottle made me nervous; it took me a few tries to pop the cork off properly, but I think Napoleon would have been proud.

ABOVE: *A leather-bound guest book was a treasure for the birthday boy to take home and remember an absolutely "pinch me" perfect party.* FOLLOWING PAGES: *The caterer, Lenôtre, packed the lunches in the individual baskets with a tin plate and silverware rolled in a Les Indiennes paisley napkin tied with raffia.*

A destination birthday party makes the added candle on a half-centennial birthday cake a little easier to blow out!

Every female guest left with a gold label popped off the top of an Amour de Deutz
Champagne bottle and tied on a black silk cord around her wrist—a beautiful
and unusual souvenir keepsake for lasting memories of a celebratory afternoon.

After lunch, guests swam in the pool and relaxed on the teak chaises covered in plush indigo- and ruby-colored Turkish towels. The guests had so much fun that the festivities unexpectedly carried on into the evening, with Ashley creating an impromptu, sunset dinner buffet, and everyone dancing barefoot around the shimmering pool until midnight! Sometimes a party can take on a life of its own—when something is working you might have to be flexible and adapt your original plan in order to suit your guests' mood. After all, no one wants to be the one to take the fizz out of a scintillating party!

SALAD OF MÂCHE,
ARUGULA, AND PINE NUTS WITH
FRENCH VINAIGRETTE

1 tablespoon minced shallot
1½ tablespoons freshly squeezed lemon juice
   (about ½ lemon)
1 teaspoon Dijon mustard
⅛ teaspoon fine-grain sea salt
3 tablespoons extra-virgin olive oil
1 teaspoon chopped fresh herbs
   (such as chives, flat-leaf parsley, or chervil)
5 bunches mâche
5 bunches arugula
½ cup pine nuts, toasted
1 cup shaved Parmigiano-Reggiano cheese

1. Combine shallot, lemon juice, mustard, and salt together in
   a medium bowl.

2. Gradually whisk in oil, then stir in herbs. Toss with the
   remaining ingredients and serve.

LEMON AND GARLIC GRILLED
CHICKEN BREAST ON BULGUR SALAD
WITH FRESH HERBS

2 tablespoons extra-virgin olive oil
6 tablespoons freshly squeezed lemon juice (about 2 lemons)
3 cloves garlic, smashed and minced
1 teaspoon finely chopped sun-dried tomato
8 organic boneless chicken breast halves, preferably skin on
2 teaspoons fine-grain sea salt
1½ teaspoons freshly ground black pepper
Toasted sesame seeds (optional, for garnish)
Bulgar Salad with Fresh Herbs (see recipe below)

1. Prepare the grill for direct-heat cooking with medium-hot
   charcoal. Combine oil, lemon juice, garlic, and sun-dried
   tomato together in a small bowl. Add chicken and let
   marinate 1 hour. Remove chicken from marinade and pat
   dry. Season both sides of chicken pieces with salt and pepper.

2. Oil the grill rack, then grill chicken, skin side down first,
   turning occasionally and moving chicken pieces around if
   flames flare up, 4 to 5 minutes or until browned and crisp
   but not burnt. Move chicken pieces to indirect heat and
   cook, turning over once, about 12 minutes or until cooked
   through. Transfer chicken to a cutting board; tent lightly
   with foil and let sit 5 minutes before slicing.

3. To serve, slice breasts and place, crisp skin side up, on top
   of the Bulgur Salad with Fresh Herbs. Garnish with
   toasted sesame seeds, if desired.

BULGUR SALAD WITH FRESH HERBS
Mint, parsley, and lemon brighten this hearty whole grain;
feel free to add chopped zucchini, asparagus, olives,
or even golden raisins.

2 cups quick-cooking bulgur
1¼ cups fresh parsley, chopped
¼ cup fresh mint, chopped
3 green onions, sliced
1½ cups chopped tomatoes
1½ cups chopped cucumber
¾ teaspoon fine-grain sea salt
¼ teaspoon freshly ground black pepper
¼ cup extra-virgin olive oil
3 tablespoons freshly squeezed lemon or orange juice
   (about 1 lemon or orange)
⅓ to ½ cup pine nuts, toasted (optional)

menu du jour

Summer Lettuce
Arugula · Mache · Parmigiano
Pine Nuts · French Dressing

Grilled Chicken Fillet
Bulgur Salad with Fresh Vegetables

Mini Beef Sandwich
Capers · Parmesan Cheese

Mini Vegetarian Sandwich

Rice Cream · Apricot Compote
Candied Fruit

1. Rinse bulgur then place in a large glass bowl and cover with cold water. Let soak 1 hour; drain and place back in bowl.

2. Add remaining ingredients and stir well to combine. Chill 1 hour. Taste and adjust by adding more salt or oil or lemon juice. Serve chilled or at room temperature.

ASSORTMENT OF SMALL SANDWICHES

A great way to let guests mix and match their own sandwiches is to provide a large platter filled with 8 to 10 mini baguettes, sliced lengthwise, and small bowls of the following: black olive tapenade, fresh soft goat cheese, sliced cornichons, sliced roast beef, Dijon mustard, mayonnaise, sliced tomatoes, lettuce, sea salt, and freshly ground black pepper.

VANILLA RICE PUDDING WITH CANDIED FRUIT AND APRICOT COMPOTE

¾ cup basmati rice
¼ teaspoon fine-grain sea salt
3 cups whole milk
1 cup heavy cream
½ cup sugar
½ vanilla bean, split lengthwise
4 to 6 tablespoons chopped candied fruit such as
  ginger or apricots (optional)
Apricot Compote (see recipe below)
Fresh apricots

1. Bring 1½ cups water, rice, and salt to a simmer in a heavy, large saucepan over medium-high heat. Reduce heat to low and cover. Simmer until water is absorbed, about 10 minutes. Add milk, cream, and sugar. Scrape in seeds from vanilla bean, and add the bean. Increase heat to medium and cook uncovered, stirring occasionally, until rice is tender and the mixture thickens slightly to a soft, creamy texture, about 35 minutes. The pudding might seem runny at first, but it will thicken up later.

2. Remove pudding from heat and discard vanilla bean. Stir in candied fruit, if desired.

3. To serve, divide pudding evenly among 8 small bowls. Serve warm with Apricot Compote and fresh apricots or press plastic wrap directly onto the surface of each pudding and chill thoroughly. Note: Pudding can be made 2 days ahead of serving. Keep refrigerated.

APRICOT COMPOTE

¾ cup sugar
3 tablespoons freshly squeezed lemon juice (about 1 lemon)
3 pounds fresh apricots, peeled, halved, and pitted
  (about 12 apricots)

1. Combine sugar and ½ cup water in a large pot over medium heat; stir and cook until sugar dissolves. Add lemon juice and apricots; stir and simmer until fruit is soft, about 15 minutes.

2. Remove from heat and let cool. Chill until ready to serve.

Lunch was beautifully presented: simple grilled chicken breast with bulgur salad; an arugula and mâche salad with pine nuts, Parmesan, and vinaigrette; and small sandwiches. For dessert we included fresh apricots and a tiny jar of rice pudding with apricot compote, sealed with a foil label embossed with "Alan's 50th."

INDIAN-INSPIRED LATE-SUMMER DINNER

Serves 8

SMOKED FIG COCKTAIL

CRISP KERALA FISH CAKES **

PORK VINDALOO SLIDERS **

KERALA SHRIMP, AVOCADO, AND MANGO SALAD **

TELLICHERRY PEPPER–CRUSTED DUCK ROAST **

BEEF BIRYANI **

CRÊPES WITH SHREDDED COCONUT,
JAGGERY, AND CARDAMOM CREAM

CHAI AND FRESH SLICED MANGOS

DINNER THEATER, BOLLYWOOD STYLE

It's a wonderful treat for a houseguest to have a party thrown in his or her honor, well . . . just because. It gives them something to look forward to and gives a host a reason to bring fun people together who might not otherwise meet. So when my dear friend Leslie Podell from San Francisco told me she was visiting, I started planning. She'd visited before, so a dinner seemed like a great a chance for her to catch up with our now-mutual friends.

Longing to entertain in my small but cozy Indian fabric–tented theater room, I ignored the challenge of the tight space and went for a glamorous take on an old-school TV tray dinner. In order to make the furniture plan work—double L-shaped banquettes and a single, central

U-shaped sofa—it required practically wedging tables in to create the seating areas. Leslie and I took the seats that would have required a guest to climb over the back of the sofa to get in and out!

I always try to seat people together who I think will enjoy each other's company, splitting up couples and connecting strangers. In this case, the close quarters made for a very spirited night, filled with lively conversation that everybody could be a part of. Fitting, considering how Leslie and I had met: eavesdropping on each another while sitting at separate—but close—tables in Italy.

The dinner by Chef Asha Gomez, of Cardamom Hill and Spice Route Supper Club, featured flavors from the Kerala region of India, each dish brilliant and exotic. The food was spicy, light, and fresh—six-spice beef biryani, a rice dish served in small, blue Staub pots, and melt-in-your-mouth-tender duck. We all took seconds, and some even had third helpings!

After dinner we sipped smoked fig cocktails from multicolored Moroccan tea glasses and worked on an intricate, Indian-inspired wooden jigsaw puzzle from Liberty Puzzle. With the hum of an Indian movie playing in the background, it was as if we'd all taken a luxurious trip to the Land of Enlightenment for a night.

ABOVE: *Hand-torn deckle-edge place cards with names elaborately written in a burgundy ink were accented with a simple sprig of rosemary tied with raffia.* OPPOSITE: *Since there were so many courses on the dinner-party menu, I planned ahead and borrowed a set of plates from a friend to mix with my already assorted settings. After all, India is all about a delirious jumble of contrasting colors and patterns. Inexpensive red water glasses and my favorite napkins, embroidered with monogrammed carnation stems and leaves, tied the exotic table together.*

Dining on tables tucked into intimate corners in a luxurious, fabric-tented room felt like dinner aboard the Orient Express.

OPPOSITE: *The card tables, covered with tea-stained Suzani-print Schumacher fabric, were small and therefore demanded compact yet "high drama" decorative centerpieces: Gold-flecked votive candle holders and tightly packed mounds of carnations placed in turquoise water glasses with ethereal gold swirls did the trick! I always love how a simple flower in abundance creates visual impact.*

CRISP KERALA FISH CAKES
Yields: 16 fish cakes

3 pounds monkfish (or haddock or cod), poached and flaked
1 red bell pepper, finely chopped
1 green bell pepper, finely chopped
2 teaspoons minced fresh ginger
2 teaspoons minced fresh garlic
1 teaspoon black peppercorns, crushed
1 teaspoon sea salt
2 tablespoons mayonnaise
1 tablespoon Dijon or whole-grain mustard
3 large eggs, lightly beaten
2 cups canola or vegetable oil (for shallow frying)

1. Combine monkfish, bell peppers, ginger, garlic, peppercorns, salt, mayonnaise, and mustard in a medium-size bowl.

2. Shape mixture into 16 round patties. Dip patties in eggs, coat well, and set aside.

3. Heat oil in a skillet. Fry fish cakes for 2 minutes on each side, until crisp and golden brown. Serve immediately.

PORK VINDALOO SLIDERS

2 to 3 dried red chiles
1 teaspoon black peppercorns
1 (3-inch) stick of cinnamon
1½ teaspoons black mustard seeds
1 teaspoon fenugreek seeds
5 tablespoons white wine vinegar
1½ to 2 teaspoons sea salt
1 teaspoon brown sugar
1 cup vegetable oil
2 medium onions, peeled and finely sliced
1 (1-inch) cube fresh ginger, chopped
1 small whole head of garlic, peeled and separated
2 pounds pork tenderloin or shoulder, trimmed and cut into 1-inch cubes
1 tablespoon ground coriander
1 teaspoon turmeric
Soft dinner rolls

1. To make vindaloo paste, grind red chiles, peppercorns, cinnamon, mustard seeds, and fenugreek in a spice or coffee grinder. Put in a small bowl. Add vinegar, salt, and brown sugar and stir; set aside.

2. Heat oil in a large pot over medium heat. Add onions and fry, stirring frequently, until onions turn golden brown. Add ginger and garlic and stir for a few seconds.

3. Add pork cubes, a few at a time, browning lightly on all sides. Add coriander and turmeric. Stir another few seconds. Add vindaloo paste and 1 cup water; stir.

4. Bring to a boil, cover, and simmer, stirring occasionally, 1 hour or until pork is tender.

5. To serve, pile on soft dinner rolls (my Atlanta favorite: Holeman & Finch Bread Co. rolls).

OPPOSITE: *Asha Gomez, a chef known for a smile as warm as her disposition, created a gastronomic fusion of traditional Indian cooking mixed with fresh herbs and produce for an inventive interpretation of modern Indian cuisine. Her spice tray filled with colorful herbs and spices included chile powder, turmeric powder, cardamom pods, garam masala, cumin seeds, coriander powder, and star anise and cloves, which kept our palates on high alert, anticipating every course!*

1. Combine mangos, tomatoes, and papaya in a small bowl. Season with salt and pepper to taste and a drizzle of olive oil. Reserve.

2. Heat coconut oil in a medium-size pot over medium-high heat; add curry leaves and chile powder, garlic powder, turmeric, peppercorns, and salt; stir 1 minute. Add shrimp and mix well until shrimp is coated with all the spices. Cook 8 to 10 minutes.

3. Divide mango-tomato-papaya salad among 8 individual serving plates and top each serving with shrimp.

TELLICHERRY PEPPER–CRUSTED DUCK ROAST

8 cardamom pods, cracked open, outer pods discarded
6 whole cloves
2 (1-inch) sticks of cinnamon
5 pounds duck legs
4 tablespoons sliced fresh ginger
14 cloves garlic, sliced
4 small, hot green chiles, chopped
14 fresh curry leaves
2 tablespoons black peppercorns, crushed
½ cup grapeseed oil
4 medium onions, sliced

1. Grind cardamom, cloves, and cinnamon together in a spice or coffee grinder. Reserve.

2. Place duck in a wide, heavy-bottomed pot; add ground spices and ginger, garlic, chiles, curry leaves, peppercorns, and 6 cups water. Cover and cook over low heat about 1 hour, or until the duck is tender and the gravy has been reduced to about 2 cups.

3. Remove from heat. Take duck from the pan and reserve the gravy.

4. Heat oil in a large pan and fry onions until they are golden brown, 8 to 10 minutes; remove and set aside.

5. In same oil used for cooking onions, fry duck pieces until brown; set aside. Pour the gravy into the oil and add the fried onions; simmer 5 minutes or until gravy has thickened.

6. Add duck and coat with gravy. Serve immediately.

KERALA SHRIMP, AVOCADO, AND MANGO SALAD

4 mangos, diced or sliced
4 tomatoes, diced or sliced
1 medium papaya, diced or sliced
Sea salt and freshly ground black pepper
Olive oil, for drizzling
5 tablespoons coconut oil
8 fresh curry leaves
2 teaspoons chile powder
2 teaspoons garlic powder
1 teaspoon turmeric
1 teaspoon crushed black peppercorns
1 teaspoon sea salt
2 pounds large shrimp (16 to 18 count), peeled and deveined, with tails still on

BEEF BIRYANI

RICE

4 tablespoons ghee (clarified butter)
4 cups uncooked long-grain rice, preferably basmati
3 (1-inch) sticks of cinnamon
1 tablespoon sea salt

BEEF

¼ cup vegetable oil
3 red onions, thinly sliced
1 tablespoon ginger paste
2 tablespoons garlic paste
3 small, hot green chiles
1 cup plain yogurt
1 teaspoon ground turmeric
1 teaspoon chile powder
8 cardamom pods, crushed
6 whole cloves
3 pounds top round beef, cut into 1-inch pieces
1 cup chopped cilantro
½ cup chopped mint leaves

2 teaspoons sea salt
1 teaspoon ghee (for garnish)
1 cup cashews, coarsely chopped (for garnish)
2 cup raisins (for garnish)
8 plum tomatoes, quartered (for garnish)

1. To prepare rice, heat ghee in a large pot; add rice and cinnamon and sauté for a few minutes, until rice is well coated with ghee.

2. Add 8 cups water and salt and cook, uncovered, until water boils; reduce heat and cook on low 15 minutes. Reserve.

3. To prepare beef, heat oil in a large pan; add onions and fry 3 to 5 minutes, or until onions turn golden brown. Add ginger paste, garlic paste, and chiles; fry 1 minute, stirring continuously. Add yogurt and stir 1 minute. Add turmeric, chile powder, cardamom, and cloves. Fry this mixture for a few minutes, stirring occasionally to prevent spices from sticking to pan.

4. Add beef and stir until meat is coated with spice mixture. Add cilantro, mint, salt, and 1 cup water. Simmer 1 hour, adding more water as needed, until meat is fork tender. Reserve.

5. To assemble Beef Biryani, preheat oven to 300°F. Sauté raisins and cashews in a medium frying pan for 2 to 4 minutes in the ghee. Reserve.

6. Divide rice into 3 portions. Spread one portion to cover the bottom of a deep, ovenproof, 10-inch square dish. Cover rice with half the cooked beef. Spread another layer of rice on top and then layer with the rest of beef. Finally, top meat with the last portion of rice. Bake 20 minutes.

7. Garnish Beef Biryani with raisin and cashew mixture, and plum tomatoes.

A FALL HARVEST–INSPIRED MENU

Serves 8

BLOOD ORANGE OLD FASHIONED**

SWEET POTATO AND PEEKYTOE CRAB TARTLETS
WITH LEMON VINAIGRETTE

BISCUITS WITH PIMENTO CHEESE AND COUNTRY HAM

YAYA EGGPLANT FRIES WITH TABASCO
AND POWDERED SUGAR **

PARSNIP BISQUE WITH CORNMEAL-FRIED OYSTERS
AND POMEGRANATE SYRUP **

FUDGE FARMS PORK CHOP WITH STONE-GROUND GRITS
AND SMOKY BRUSSELS SPROUTS **

CRANBERRY-PECAN TART **

S'MORES **

BOURBON AND BONFIRE CHIC:
A CHEF'S TABLE IN THE KITCHEN

Embracing the wonderfully crisp autumn weather and hoping to celebrate being outdoors to catch the vibrant leaves at their blazing colorful peak, I invited a small group of friends over for an autumnal fête and fall harvest dinner. Invitations called for "bonfire chic." It gave everyone a chance to finally break out the thick sweaters, cozy jackets, and corduroys that mark the start of this season. Blood Orange Old Fashioneds were made to order—using Bulleit Bourbon—by the bartender working behind an outdoor bar that was the centerpiece of the small patio overlooking the blazing bonfire in the

fire pit. The bar was draped in rough burlap fabric to blend into the season's natural backdrop and decorated with a pair of overscale lanterns fashioned out of reclaimed wood, making it chinoiserie-meets-rustic-chic. Guests enjoyed savory appetizers served from woven-twig-branch trays.

Since the kitchen is the heart of most homes and a natural gathering spot for any party, I turned the large center island into a custom chef's table, flanked with bar-height Chiavari chairs. Once it became dark, guests made their way indoors to the kitchen, where they were treated to a huge surprise.

Dinner was prepared by the famed and beloved Iron Chef Kevin Rathbun, owner of the popular Atlanta restaurants Rathbun's, Krog Bar, KR Steak Bar, and Kevin Rathbun Steak. He was in his chef's toque working culinary pyrotechnics on the persimmon Le Cornue range. It was a thrill for the guests to watch a

ABOVE: *Always inspired by using what is readily available and seasonal, I scaled the trees in our yard with a pair of tree clippers. Large terra-cotta urns decorated with pebbles and river rocks held branches of loosely arranged fall-toned Japanese maple branches and glossy evergreen magnolia branches.* OPPOSITE: *Dinner was in honor of David York, who established Sophie's Uptown, a delightful* chien-*friendly café and bakery in Atlanta, whose proceeds are directed toward animal rescue services and humane shelters.*

BLOOD ORANGE
OLD FASHIONED

16 to 24 brown sugar cubes (such as Sugar in the Raw)
Blood orange bitters (see Resources)
16 ounces Bulleit Bourbon or other good-quality,
   artisanal bourbon
32 ounces freshly squeezed blood orange juice
   (available seasonally, or substitute orange juice)
Thinly sliced blood orange wheels and/or thickly
   sliced zest of blood orange, for garnish
Lime-flavored sparkling water
8 double old-fashioned glasses and ice cubes

1. Put 2 or 3 brown sugar cubes in each double old-
   fashioned glass; soak with blood orange bitters and
   let dissolve. (Helpful hint: Doing this a couple hours
   ahead of time allows the sugar to dissolve and saves
   time when making drinks.)

2. Fill a large pitcher with Bourbon and blood orange
   juice. Stir to combine.

3. To serve individual drinks, fill a glass with ice. Pour
   blood orange–Bourbon mixture over the ice and
   top with a splash of sparkling water. Garnish with a
   blood orange wheel and/or blood orange zest.

*Preparing the glasses ahead of time with rough-cut,
pure cane sugar cubes soaked with blood orange bitters
allowed the bartender to add ice and fill each glass as
needed from a big pitcher of premade Blood Orange Old
Fashioned mix with Bourbon—topped with a splash of
lime-flavored sparkling water just before serving!*

true culinary artist. Chef Kevin's rich menu, consisting of grilled pork chops served over creamy grits and Brussels sprouts, made even more decadent with a garnish of thick-cut smoky bacon, definitely evoked the theme of fall harvest. Dessert was a sensational Cranberry-Pecan Tart with sweet-cream ice cream drizzled with a cinnamon sauce. It was perfectly fall-themed comfort food, which in my opinion means happiness. Comfort food is a favorite pick of mine for parties because it typically thrills the men and gives the women a chance to indulge a little more than they might ordinarily. Adorable dog-themed cupcakes with names iced on tiny marzipan bones served as place cards and as a nod to the guest of honor. A personal touch always makes guests feel at home, and since it's been said that most people tend to resemble their dogs (I just act like mine), I did my best to match the various dog faces to each guest's name. After the delicious repast, we all headed back outside to enjoy the brisk and invigorating night. Rolled-up Polartec blankets were placed on the Adirondeck chairs, ensuring that everyone kept toasty and warm as they sat around the roaring bonfire. Gourmet s'mores made with flavored marshmallows, dark chocolate, and homemade graham crackers added the perfect touch of nostalgia and an ideal ending to a harvest feast under the sliver of the crescent moon.

Unmatched terra-cotta pots of clipped boxwood balls and small vases of vibrant orange mums mixed with orange glass votives created the decorative elements around the island dining spot. Terra-cotta-colored napkins with white crochet-edged trim and Italian pottery plates painted with boxwoods in terra-cotta pots and trellis patterns added to the rustic feel, while inexpensive green water glasses mixed with plain crystal wineglasses tied the casual look together with rustic elegance.

2. Heat oil in a large pot to 350°F. Set out three bowls. In one bowl, mix flour and salt together. In the second bowl, whisk together milk and eggs. Put bread crumbs in the third bowl.

3. Dredge eggplant in flour and salt, shaking off any excess flour. Then dip in egg and milk mixture. Then coat with bread crumbs.

4. Fry eggplant in batches until golden brown and crisp, turning occasionally, 2 to 3 minutes. Drain on a paper-towel-lined plate. Dust eggplant fries with 2 tablespoons powdered sugar immediately before serving and serve with Tabasco–powdered sugar sauce.

PARSNIP BISQUE WITH CORNMEAL-FRIED OYSTERS AND POMEGRANATE SYRUP

2 pounds parsnips, peeled and coarsely chopped
1 coarsely chopped yellow onion
¼ cup extra-virgin olive oil
Kosher or sea salt
1 teaspoon freshly ground black pepper
4 cups chicken stock
1 cup heavy cream
2 tablespoons unsalted butter
Cornmeal-Fried Oysters (see recipe below)
Pomegranate Syrup and reserved pomegranate seeds
  (see recipe below)

1. Preheat the oven to 350°F.

2. Combine parsnips, onion, oil, salt, and pepper in a bowl; stir to coat vegetables evenly and transfer the vegetables to a sheet pan. Roast until tender, about 20 minutes, stirring occasionally. Transfer vegetables to a soup pot and add stock and cream. Bring to a boil, then lower heat and simmer until vegetables are tender, about 5 minutes.

3. Transfer mixture to a blender and add butter. Carefully puree until smooth, being cautious to not burn yourself with the hot liquid. Season to taste with additional salt, if needed.

4. Evenly divide bisque among 8 bowls, then top each serving with 1 fried oyster, a drizzle of Pomegranate Syrup, and a few reserved pomegranate seeds. The soup is also delicious alone or with crisp fried onions, sautéed mushrooms, and the like.

YAYA EGGPLANT FRIES WITH TABASCO AND POWDERED SUGAR

½ cup powdered sugar, plus 2 tablespoons for garnish
½ cup Tabasco sauce
6 cups canola oil
1 ½ cups all-purpose flour
1 teaspoon salt
2 cups milk
6 large eggs, beaten
4 cups seasoned bread crumbs
2 large eggplant, peeled and cut into 1 x 1 x 3-inch fries

1. Whisk together powdered sugar and Tabasco sauce to make a sauce; reserve.

CORNMEAL-FRIED OYSTERS

3 cups canola oil
1 large egg, beaten
¼ cup milk
8 freshly shucked oysters
½ cup yellow cornmeal
½ cup all-purpose flour
1 teaspoon cayenne pepper
2 teaspoons fine-grain salt
1 teaspoon freshly ground black pepper

1. Heat oil in a large pot to 350°F.

2. Whisk egg and milk together in a large bowl and add oysters.

3. In another large bowl, whisk together cornmeal, flour, cayenne, salt, and black pepper. Transfer oysters from egg mixture to cornmeal mixture and dredge, shaking off any excess.

4. Fry oysters in oil, turning occasionally, until light brown and crisp, about 2 minutes. Drain on a paper-towel-lined plate and serve immediately.

POMEGRANATE SYRUP

2 tablespoons fresh pomegranate juice
(about ½ pomegranate, or use commercially available pomegranate juice and omit garnish using pomegranate seeds)
4 tablespoons red-wine vinegar
3 tablespoons sugar
Pinch of kosher or sea salt

1. Cut pomegranate in half. Remove seeds from one half and set them aside for the garnish.

2. Juice the other half into a small pot and add vinegar, sugar, and salt. Bring mixture to a boil and cook until it becomes thick and syrupy, about 4 minutes. Set aside to cool and reserve.

FUDGE FARMS PORK CHOP WITH STONE-GROUND GRITS AND SMOKY BRUSSELS SPROUTS

½ cup kosher salt
3 tablespoons black peppercorns
3 bay leaves
1 teaspoon juniper berries
1 teaspoon red chile flakes
1 cup roughly chopped yellow onion
5 cloves garlic, smashed
8 (14-ounce) pork chops, Frenched
Smoky Brussels Sprouts (see recipe below)
Stone-Ground Grits (see recipe below)

1. To prepare brine for pork chops, combine 2 quarts water, salt, peppercorns, bay leaves, juniper berries, chile flakes, onion, and garlic together in a large pot; bring to a boil and cook 2 minutes.

2. Let cool, then pour brine over pork chops. Chill them in the refrigerator for 24 hours.

2. When ready to cook pork chops, heat a grill to medium-high. Place chops on grill and cook to medium or until a thermometer inserted in center reads 135°F. Serve with Smoky Brussels Sprouts and Stone-Ground Grits.

SMOKY BRUSSELS SPROUTS

1½ pounds Brussels sprouts
8 ounces thick-cut bacon, pancetta, or uncured ham
3 tablespoons olive oil
2 teaspoons sea salt
1 teaspoon freshly ground black pepper
¾ cup chicken stock
½ cup unsalted butter
1 tablespoon chopped sage

1. Cut bacon into ½-inch slices or cubes.

2. Sauté over medium heat 3 to 4 minutes or until fully cooked. Reserve.

3. To cook Brussels sprouts, preheat oven to 350°F.

4. Trim ends of Brussels sprouts and cut each in half. Toss with oil, salt, and pepper. Place Brussels sprouts on a baking sheet in an even layer and roast about 20 minutes or until tender.

5. Heat a large sauté pan over medium-high heat; brown bacon 2 minutes. Add roasted Brussels sprouts to pan. Add stock, butter, and sage and simmer 3 to 5 minutes. Adjust seasoning to taste and serve.

STONE-GROUND GRITS

2 tablespoons unsalted butter
2 tablespoons chopped shallot
1 cup stone-ground grits
½ cup fresh corn, pureed
2 cups chicken or corn stock
¾ cup heavy cream
2 teaspoons kosher salt
½ to ¾ teaspoon cracked black pepper

1. Melt 1 tablespoon butter in a sauté pan. Add shallot and cook about 1 minute.

2. Add grits, corn puree, and stock; simmer, stirring constantly, 30 minutes.

3. Add cream, salt, pepper, and remaining 1 tablespoon butter and simmer 10 more minutes. Adjust seasoning to taste and serve.

OPPOSITE: *Chef Kevin Rathbun adds a last-minute sprinkle of salt to the soup just before preparing to serve it.*
BELOW: *Creating a "chef's table" around the large center island was a wonderful, easy way to entertain in the kitchen, especially since everyone usually ends up there anyway!*

CRANBERRY-PECAN TART

TART DOUGH
¼ cup powdered sugar
⅛ teaspoon salt
⅓ cup unsalted butter
I large egg
¾ cup all-purpose flour

FILLING
¼ cup unsalted butter
3 large eggs
½ cup granulated sugar
½ cup light brown sugar
¾ cup corn syrup
I teaspoon vanilla extract
¼ teaspoon sea salt
I cup fresh cranberries
I¼ cups pecan halves

1. To make tart dough, sift together powdered sugar and salt into a large bowl; cream together with butter using a hand mixer. Add egg and blend, then add flour, ¼ cup at a time, blending after each addition. Scrape the sides of the bowl and add remaining flour and mix until just combined.

2. Form into a disk and refrigerate 30 minutes or until ready to use.

3. To make filling, melt butter and combine with the eggs, sugars, corn syrup, vanilla, and salt until smooth; reserve.

4. On a lightly floured surface, roll tart dough out into a circle, about 10 inches in diameter and approximately ⅛ inch thick. Line a tart pan with the dough and set aside to chill in the refrigerator at least 20 minutes. (This resting period will ensure that the shell does not shrink during baking.)

5. Preheat oven to 350°F.

6. Bake the tart shell about 15 minutes or until it is just starting to turn golden. Remove from oven and let cool.

7. Arrange cranberries on the bottom of tart shell and top with pecans. Pour filling over the cranberries and pecans until it reaches just to the top of the shell.

8. Bake 40 to 50 minutes, or until center is set and jiggles slightly. If crust begins to get too dark, lightly cover with foil until tart is set.

S'MORES

Assorted chocolate bars (dark, milk, and white)
Assorted marshmallows (strawberry, peppermint,
  chocolate, and vanilla)
Graham Crackers (recipe below)

Have your guests toast marshmallows over the fire
or grill. Sandwich with a slab of chocolate between
two graham crackers.

GRAHAM CRACKERS

1¼ cups graham flour
½ cup all-purpose flour
6 tablespoons dark
  brown sugar
¾ tablespoon baking powder
½ tablespoon baking soda
½ tablespoon kosher salt

⅛ tablespoon
  ground cinnamon
6 tablespoons cold
  unsalted butter
4½ tablespoons molasses
3 tablespoons whole milk
½ tablespoon vanilla extract

1. Place flours, brown sugar, baking powder, baking soda,
   salt, and cinnamon in a food processor and pulse until
   combined. Dice butter and add, pulsing until the
   mixture has the consistency of a very fine crumb. Add

molasses, milk, and vanilla and process until the dough
forms a ball. Press ball into a flat disk, wrap in plastic,
and refrigerate 30 minutes.

2. Preheat oven to 350°F.

3. Unwrap chilled dough and place on a large piece of
   parchment paper; top with a second sheet of parchment
   paper. Roll dough out until it is ⅛ inch thick.

4. Place the rolled dough, still between the parchment paper
   sheets, onto a half sheet pan. Remove the top sheet of
   parchment paper and cut the dough, using
   a perforated cracker cutter or pizza cutter, into 2-inch-
   square pieces by making a grid of vertical and horizontal
   cuts. Trim off any excess. Using the perforated cracker
   cutter or a fork, poke holes all over the top of the dough.

5. Bake until crackers are done, about 25 minutes, making
   sure to rotate pan after 10 minutes.

6. Remove from oven and place on a cooling rack. Once
   crackers have cooled, break into individual pieces and store
   in an airtight container.

AN ELEGANT DINNER WITH A SPLASH OF SASS

Serves 8

BELLE OF THE BALL **

FARM SALAD OF BUTTER LETTUCE, HOUSE-CURED BACON, SOFT-POACHED FARM EGG, AND VINAIGRETTE

LIGHTLY CURED NORTH GEORGIA TROUT WITH FENNEL, CUCUMBERS, AND TARRAGON **

WOOD-GRILLED MAGRET DUCK BREAST WITH ELLIJAY APPLE COMPOTE AND CELERY **

CHOCOLATE-PECAN PIE WITH TOASTED MARSHMALLOW CHANTILLY CREAM **

SOUTHERN HOSPITALITY FOR A TRUE GENTLEMAN

It was a dream come true: teaming up with Neiman Marcus to host a dinner in honor of Oscar de la Renta. That the dinner benefitted Children's Healthcare of Atlanta—an institution that had provided critical care to my middle child, who had had a lengthy stay there following an accident—made it even more significant and special.

It was a hard sell convincing people that I wanted to have one of the world's greatest designers sit at a table covered in burlap and linen with humble vases of dahlias . . . and then serve him (*gasp*) Southern food! But reasoning that everyone else would try to impress Mr. de la Renta with overly fancy and fussy presentations, I remained true to my mother's advice to be myself and gave him an evening of simplicity that highlighted what I treasure most about Georgia.

The week of the party, Atlanta experienced floods of almost biblical proportions. And I do mean floods! It poured for over a week. Since the party was to be held outside, and there was no room in the house to accommodate a sixty-foot table, extreme measures had to taken. We put up a giant tent that covered the entire lawn, which prevented more water from soaking into the grass. We also set up huge golf course fans to dry the grounds. As if in answer to prayers and homage to the great Mr. de la Renta, the morning of the event the rain miraculously stopped, the sun came out, and the tent came down.

Guests sipped cava, a sparkling Spanish wine, while an acoustic flamenco guitarist played in the courtyard. It was my little tribute to Mr. de la Renta's days in Spain when he worked with renowned couturier Cristóbal Balenciaga. Everyone was delighted that Mr. de la Renta greeted each of them personally, and many ladies were charmed by his gift and ability to make each woman feel as if he had designed her dress especially for her. Out of respect and as a sign of adoration, many were clad in the guest of honor's designs.

One large table covered in burlap cloth, topped with wheat grasses and surrounded by fruitwood Chiavari chairs created a naturalistic element, almost as if the table were floating into the garden.

When I entertain I want the event to be both magical and memorable, regardless of whether it's for two or two hundred people. The incredible chef and restaurateur Anne Quatrano, who, together with her husband and partner, Clifford Harris, runs a mini-epicurean empire in Atlanta (Bacchanalia, Abattoir, Quinones, Star Provisions, and Floataway Café), jumped on board immediately to create a superb Southern and seasonal menu featuring locally farmed produce, north Georgia trout, and crisp apples from Elijay.

To personalize the table, I used many of my own accent pieces, mixing them with William Yeoward crystal and Herend China loaned from Neiman Marcus. I also borrowed silverware from friends and family and mixed these with my own to create a very quirky but charming ensemble. Each plate was topped with a crisply folded napkin emblazoned with what is now my signature, a monogrammed R, in a boxwood pattern custommade by Leontine Linens. Simple vases filled with white dahlias from the north Georgia mountains were mixed with small glasses of wheat grass to create bold punches of color on the table; exactly what I envisioned, thanks to my very favorite floral designer, Michal Evans of Michal Evans Floral. Beeswax candles were anchored with coffee beans in beautifully etched glass hurricanes. Looking down at the softly illuminated table, I knew the evening was a success when I saw guests laughing and having a wonderful time. More important, one long table ensured that everyone could say they sat with Oscar de la Renta at dinner!

OPPOSITE: *Mr. de la Renta personally greeted each guest during the cocktail hour and was genuinely thrilled to receive a signed copy of a book on gardening, one of his many passions.*

BELLE OF THE BALL

Mint leaves (for ice cubes)
Ginger beer
16 ounces Belle de Brillet, a pear liqueur
1½ ounces freshly squeezed lemon juice (about 1 lemon)
Sprigs of mint (for garnish)
8 stemless wineglasses

1. Fill ice cube trays with water and add mint leaves.
   Freeze overnight.

2. To serve individual drinks, fill a stemless wineglass half
   full with ginger beer and add 2 ounces Belle de Brillet.
   Add a squeeze of fresh lemon juice to taste and 2 or 3
   large mint ice cubes. Serve garnished with a sprig of mint.

OPPOSITE AND FOLLOWING PAGES: *Coffee beans
in the bottom of clear glass hurricanes anchored groups
of beeswax candles, which filled the air with a
warm, inviting aroma and provided subtle ambient
light for dining as it grew dark.*

LIGHTLY CURED NORTH GEORGIA TROUT WITH FENNEL, CUCUMBERS, AND TARRAGON

16 (6-ounce) cleaned trout fillets, with the skin on
   and split lengthwise (8 trout)
¼ cup sugar
¼ cup salt
Finely grated zest of 1 lemon
1 teaspoon chopped chervil, plus 1 tablespoon leaves
1 teaspoon chopped chives
1 teaspoon chopped tarragon, plus 1 tablespoon leaves
2 tablespoons extra-virgin olive oil
1 tablespoon butter
1 English cucumber, peeled, seeded,
   and cut into 1-inch batons
1 bulb fennel, shaved on a mandolin slicer
3 tablespoons freshly squeezed lemon juice
   (about 1 lemon)
Sea salt and freshly ground black pepper

1. Rinse each trout fillet and pat dry.

2. Combine sugar, salt, lemon zest, chervil, chives, and
   tarragon in the bowl of a food processor. Blend until well
   combined, about 1 minute. Rub this herb mixture onto
   flesh-side of each fillet and let sit 20 minutes.

3. In large sauté pan, heat 1 tablespoon olive oil and butter
   over medium heat. Add trout skin side down and sear until
   crispy. Turn and cook for 2 minutes.

4. Combine the cucumber, fennel, herbs, lemon juice, and
   remaining tablespoon extra-virgin olive oil. Season with
   salt and pepper to taste.

5. To serve, place 2 pieces of trout fillet, to make one whole
   filet, on each plate. Garnish with the salad of cucumber,
   fennel, and herbs.

WOOD-GRILLED MAGRET DUCK BREAST WITH ELLIJAY APPLE COMPOTE AND CELERY

1 cup sugar
⅔ cup sea salt
1 cup basil leaves
1 cup mint leaves
2 tablespoons chopped rosemary
2 teaspoons grated orange zest
2 cloves garlic, peeled
4 Magret duck breasts, trimmed, leaving ¼ inch fat
Apple Compote (see recipe below)
Thinly sliced celery and celery leaves tossed with
   olive oil and lemon (for garnish)

1. Combine sugar, salt, basil, mint, rosemary, orange zest, and
   garlic together in a food processor fitted with a stainless-
   steel blade. Pulse until incorporated.

2. Score the fat side of duck across the skin. Rub both sides of
   duck with the basil-mint rub and let sit uncovered in the
   refrigerator overnight.

3. When duck is ready to cook, heat a charcoal grill or a nonstick pan over the stovetop to medium heat. Sear the duck breast, fat side down, 5 minutes. Turn and cook 4 more minutes for medium-rare meat.

4. To serve, slice one half of each breast into thin slices and arrange the slices and the remaining unsliced portion on a plate. Serve with Apple Compote and garnish with celery.

APPLE COMPOTE
¼ cup white wine vinegar
1 cup sugar
½ teaspoon salt
4 Fuji apples, peeled and finely diced

1. Bring ½ cup water, vinegar, sugar, and salt to a simmer; add apples and cook 1 minute.

2. Remove apples and reduce the cooking liquid to about half. Reserve both.

CHOCOLATE-PECAN PIE WITH TOASTED MARSHMALLOW CHANTILLY CREAM
Yields: 8 individual tarts

TART DOUGH
½ cup unsalted butter, softened
½ cup powdered sugar
1 large egg yolk
¾ teaspoon vanilla extract
1¼ cups all-purpose flour, sifted
¼ cup cocoa powder

CHOCOLATE FILLING
2 cups heavy cream
8 ounces Callebaut or Valrhona 66% chocolate
2 tablespoons cold butter
½ teaspoon sea salt

MARSHMALLOW CHANTILLY CREAM
1 cup sugar
1 cup glucose, plus ¼ cup for whipping with egg whites
½ cup egg whites
2 teaspoons vanilla extract
1 cup toasted Georgia pecans (for garnish)

1. To make tart dough, combine butter and sugar in the bowl of a stand mixer with a paddle attachment; mix on medium speed. Add egg yolk and vanilla extract. Sift flour and cocoa together and slowly add to bowl and mix. Place dough on counter and form into a flat disk; refrigerate at least 1 hour.

2. Preheat oven to 300°F.

3. To make tart shell, on a lightly floured surface, roll the tart dough out to approximately ⅛ inch thick. Use the dough to fill 8 individual 4-inch tart pans. Blind bake for 8 minutes. Let cool. Can be stored up to 4 days.

4. To make chocolate filling, heat cream in a medium-size pan over medium heat until just warm. Pour into a bowl with the chocolate and stir to melt.

5. Add butter and stir, then add salt. Cool slightly, then fill baked tart shells. Tart shells can be made the day before and stored in a covered container at room temperature.

6. To make marshmallow chantilly cream, combine sugar, ½ cup water, and 1 cup glucose in a stainless-steel saucepan; heat until a candy thermometer reaches 240°F. Keep warm.

7. Whip egg whites and ¼ cup glucose in a medium-size bowl until fluffy and shiny but not dry. Add vanilla to egg whites. Continue whipping, adding hot sugar and glucose mixture, until light and fluffy.

8. To serve, top each tart with marshmallow chantilly cream and garnish with pecans. Toast marshmallow cream with a kitchen torch or in the broiler.

ABOVE: *Chef Anne Quatrano samples dessert.*

A VIETNAMESE-INSPIRED LUNCHEON

Serves 8

HIBISCUS SODA **

GARDEN VEGETABLE SALAD WITH
PICKLED GINGER VINAIGRETTE

VERMICELLI SALAD BOWL WITH LIME VINAIGRETTE **

MISO-GLAZED TROUT WITH SAUTÉED SPINACH,
SHIITAKE LEEK BROTH, AND SHAVED TURNIP SALAD **

FIVE-SPICE FRUIT SALAD WITH
HONEYSUCKLE AND GINGER SORBET **

LADIES WHO LUNCH

A stylish friend deserves a stylish welcome. When fashion designer Rachel Roy came to visit, I hosted a luncheon so she could meet my friends and fellow fashionistas. The night before the luncheon, I set out the table settings and ingredients I would need for cooking and put sticky notes on everything so I would remember it all in the morning. Before going to bed, I whipped up some hibiscus syrup for the sodas. I made the madeleine batter and spooned it into trays (a Parisian trick for getting the perfect little humps), and placed the trays in the refrigerator so I could bake them the following day during lunch and serve them fresh from the oven.

PREVIOUS PAGES: *Spiky orange pincushion protea, picked up during a last-minute run to Whole Foods and abundantly bunched into an elegant leaf-etched crystal vase, along with the gomphrena clipped from my garden gathered in tiny silver garden pails scattered about the table, created a visual contrast with minimum fuss or expense. I always prefer to use masses of something more common and splurge on a vase I can use and enjoy many times over.* ABOVE AND OPPOSITE: *The vibrant color on this table was not in my original plan, but sometimes color is more important than simplicity. Don't be afraid to make a last-minute change to give a table some extra zing. Adding a festive touch doesn't take that much more effort and makes guests feel extra special.*

HIBISCUS SODA

2 $\frac{1}{3}$ cups sugar
3 cups hibiscus flowers
1 $\frac{1}{2}$ cups freshly squeezed lemon juice (8 to 10 lemons)
6 cups sparkling water

1. Combine 6 cups water and sugar in a saucepan and bring
   to a boil, stirring constantly, until sugar dissolves and the
   liquid becomes clear; reduce heat and simmer, stirring
   continually, 5 to 10 minutes.

2. Add hibiscus flowers. Remove from heat and cover,
   letting sit until the simple syrup reaches room
   temperature. Strain and discard hibiscus flowers.

3. Combine lemon juice with cooled simple syrup
   mixture in a large pitcher. Add sparkling water
   to the pitcher and stir.

NOTE
Tequila, rum, vodka, or gin complement this soda
beautifully; add 2 ounces of your desired liquor per glass.

When I wandered to the breakfast room in the morning, my jaw dropped. My youngest son was adding his final "flourishes" to the table I'd set the night before. He was clutching some of my prized Baccarat Mosaique glasses, so I kept silent, fearful he would drop them. After noticing me, he said, beaming with pride, "I didn't think it looked special and you always tell people it's better to use the good stuff instead of letting it collect dust!" The Roberta Roller Rabbit linens were the only things he hadn't replaced. He had put out vintage persimmon wineglasses and swapped the white china for turquoise-bordered china. But he was onto something. It looked more festive! Inspired by his work, I added place cards decorated with hand-painted birds, which I had been saving for a special occasion.

Rachel and guests gathered around the table sipping hibiscus lemonade and Blackbird Vineyards rosé. We savored the light, refreshing, summery menu. However, once I started serving, I realized that, despite my preplanning, I didn't have a ladle for the Shiitake-Leek Broth, which was to go over the trout dish. A master of improvisation, I used a teapot and drizzled away, and my guests commented on the clever way I served the broth.

After an easy-to-prepare dessert of Chinese five-spice salad with honeysuckle-scented ice cream and madeleines dusted in powdered sugar, the Southern girls taught Rachel a childhood indulgence: how to get the honeysuckle nectar from the blossom's end. Most of us grew up with it in our yards and enjoyed the trip down memory lane. Rosé in hand, we retreated to a shady spot on the patio for a lazy afternoon of girl talk.

<hr />

PREVIOUS PAGES: *For a spin on a summertime favorite—lemonade—I added my own personal special twist: a splash of gin and touch of hibiscus. Yes, please!* OPPOSITE: *Rachel Roy loved the hand-painted bird place cards and kept hers as a memento of our lunch.*

VERMICELLI SALAD BOWL
WITH LIME VINAIGRETTE

8 ounces vermicelli noodles
3 tablespoons sesame oil
1 tablespoon unsalted butter
8 ounces red pearl onions, peeled
Sea salt and freshly ground black pepper
16 ounces exotic mushrooms, such as maitake, shiitake,
    chanterelle, or cèpes
1 bunch watercress
2 heads savoy cabbage
4 green onions, thinly sliced
¾ cup cashews, toasted and chopped
Lime Vinaigrette (see recipe below)

1. Preheat oven to 375° F.

2. Place a medium-size pot filled with water on stove and
   bring to a boil. Cook noodles in boiling water until
   tender, then drain and shock in an ice bath. Once cold,
   drain noodles and roughly chop into 1-inch pieces.

2. Heat an ovenproof skillet over medium-high heat, then
   add 1 tablespoon sesame oil and butter. When butter starts
   to foam, add pearl onions. Season with salt and pepper
   to taste; cook 2 to 3 minutes. Place pan, covered, in oven.
   Cook about 20 minutes, or until tender.

3. Remove stems and any dirt from mushrooms, using
   a damp cloth; cut into large pieces. Heat remaining
   2 tablespoons sesame oil over high heat and sauté
   mushrooms, about 10 minutes. Let cool and chop finely.
   Wash watercress and cabbage and pat dry. Set aside 12 of
   the best and biggest cabbage leaves to use as salad bowls
   and shred the remaining cabbage leaves.

4. Put noodles, pearl onions, mushrooms, watercress, shredded
   cabbage, and cashews in a bowl. Add Lime Vinaigrette
   and toss. Divide noodle salad evenly among cabbage leaves,
   garnish with green onions, and serve on a platter.

LIME VINAIGRETTE
Yields: 1½ cups
⅓ cup freshly squeezed lime juice
   (about 6 limes)
2 tablespoons rice wine vinegar
½ teaspoon Dijon mustard
Zest of 1 orange
4 teaspoons soy sauce
3 dashes of fish sauce
1 tablespoon sambal chile paste
1 cup almond oil

1. Place all the ingredients except oil in a medium-size bowl.
   Whisk by hand until thickened. Slowly drizzle in oil and
   whisk briskly until fully emulsified.

2. Store in an airtight container up to 2 weeks.

MISO-GLAZED TROUT WITH SAUTÉED
SPINACH, SHIITAKE-LEEK BROTH, AND
SHAVED TURNIP SALAD

¾ cup yellow miso paste
½ cup soy sauce
8 fresh trout fillets, pin bones removed, skin on
2 tablespoons grapeseed oil
Sautéed Spinach (see recipe below)
Shaved Turnip Salad (see recipe below)
Shiitake-Leek Broth (see recipe below)

*When the weather is hot, serving a lighter meal is preferable.
Fish, fresh vegetables, and tiny or delicate fruit-based
desserts are always flavorful, and much appreciated!
A refreshing summery drink and a chilled wine will have
guests satisfied and happy, despite the temperature.*

1. Turn broiler to high.

2. Combine miso paste and soy sauce in a bowl and mix well. Reserve.

3. Score trout skin with a knife and heat a large pan over medium-high heat. Add oil, and when the pan is barely smoking, sear trout, skin side down, about 4 minutes.

4. Transfer trout fillets to a baking sheet and brush top of fish with miso-soy glaze. Place under broiler and cook until flesh is firm, about 8 minutes.

5. To serve, place Sautéed Spinach on a plate, then place a trout fillet on top of spinach. Garnish with Shaved Turnip Salad and pour a little bit of the Shiitake-Leek Broth over the plate. Serve immediately.

SAUTÉED SPINACH
3 tablespoons unsalted butter
4 cloves garlic, thinly sliced
4 pounds spinach, washed and stems removed
Sea salt and freshly ground black pepper

1. Melt butter in a large pan over medium heat. When butter begins to foam, add garlic. Sauté 30 seconds, then add spinach.

2. Cook until just wilted; season with salt and pepper to taste and serve immediately.

SHIITAKE-LEEK BROTH
3 tablespoons sesame oil
3 ounces shiitake mushrooms
2 baby leeks, rinsed well and sliced
3 cups chicken stock
1 teaspoon wakame seaweed
1 teaspoon bonito flakes
Sea salt and freshly ground black pepper
3 tablespoons unsalted butter

1. Heat sesame oil in a medium pot over medium-high heat. Add shiitakes and cook 2 minutes, then add leeks and reduce heat to medium; sauté 3 minutes. Add stock, wakame, and bonito. Simmer 45 minutes, then strain.

2. Just before serving broth, season with salt and pepper to taste, and whisk in butter, 1 tablespoon at a time. Serve immediately.

SHAVED TURNIP SALAD
8 baby turnips
½ cup fresh cilantro leaves
Sea salt and freshly ground black pepper
1 teaspoon olive oil

1. Wash turnips and slice, using a slicer such as a mandolin slicer, as thinly as possible. Wash cilantro and pat dry.

2. Place turnips and cilantro in a bowl, season with salt and pepper to taste, then toss with oil. Serve immediately.

FIVE-SPICE FRUIT SALAD WITH HONEYSUCKLE AND GINGER SORBET

3 ripe kiwi fruit
2 bananas
2 pints strawberries
1 pint raspberries
1 pint blueberries
1 pint dewberries (or blackberries)
1 bunch of honeysuckle flowers that have not been treated with pesticide
2 tablespoons five-spice powder
¼ cup muscovado sugar (a natural brown sugar)
Ginger Sorbet (see recipe below)

1. Wash all fruit. Peel kiwi by cutting off ends and making a slit from top to bottom. Take a spoon and get inside the split and work your way around the kiwi to peel the skin off. (This will only work if the kiwi is ripe.) Peel bananas and slice. Cut tops off of strawberries and cut in half lengthwise.

2. Just before serving, place all fruit in a mixing bowl and toss with five-spice powder and muscovado sugar. Serve with Ginger Sorbet.

GINGER SORBET
1 ½ pounds sugar
½ teaspoon sorbet stabilizer (Sevagel is a popular brand and can be found on Amazon and many other online sites.)
⅓ cup freshly juiced ginger

1. Bring 6 cups water to a boil in a medium-size saucepan. Blend sugar and stabilizer together and add to boiling water. Stir and let sugar dissolve. Remove from heat and let cool, then stir in ginger juice.

2. Churn in an ice cream or sorbet maker according to manufacturer's instructions.

AN AUTHENTIC AND COMFORTING FALL MEAL

Serves 8

Chamomile-Thyme Brown Derby**

Walnut Crostini with Blue Cheese, Asian Pear,
and Fig Vin Cotto

Butternut Squash Soup Shooters **

Endive Salad with Lemon Vinaigrette**

Roast Chicken with Risotto and Mushroom Fricassee **

Brown Sugar–Sautéed Rainbow Carrots **

Holeman & Finch Fried Apple Pies
with Cinnamon Ice Cream **

DESIGNING AN AWARD-WINNING DINNER

It was only fitting that I should throw a congratulatory dinner for New York–based classicist architect Gil Schafer, winner of *Veranda* magazine's Art of Design Award, at my Atlanta home, Boxwood. Extensively and lovingly renovated with Gil's help, the English vernacular–style house designed by the esteemed architect Philip Schutze (designer of Atlanta's Swan House) was built as a replica of the original owner's childhood home in Chicago. Dara Caponigro, editor in chief of *Veranda*, and a mix of noteworthy East Coast tastemakers helped make the dinner a true celebration in a house that stands as an emblem of Gil's craftsmanship.

ABOVE AND OPPOSITE: *A palette of turquoise and brown tones was chosen for this occasion so that the colors would coordinate nicely in either an indoor or outdoor setting. Even the place cards and the flowers, julep cups filled with chocolate-brown cosmos, matched the rich, autumnal color scheme. A mixed place-setting of vintage turquoise and gilt-rim plates from auction and a striking, modern chinoiserie set looked perfect on a table covering made from a Charlotte Moss fabric.*

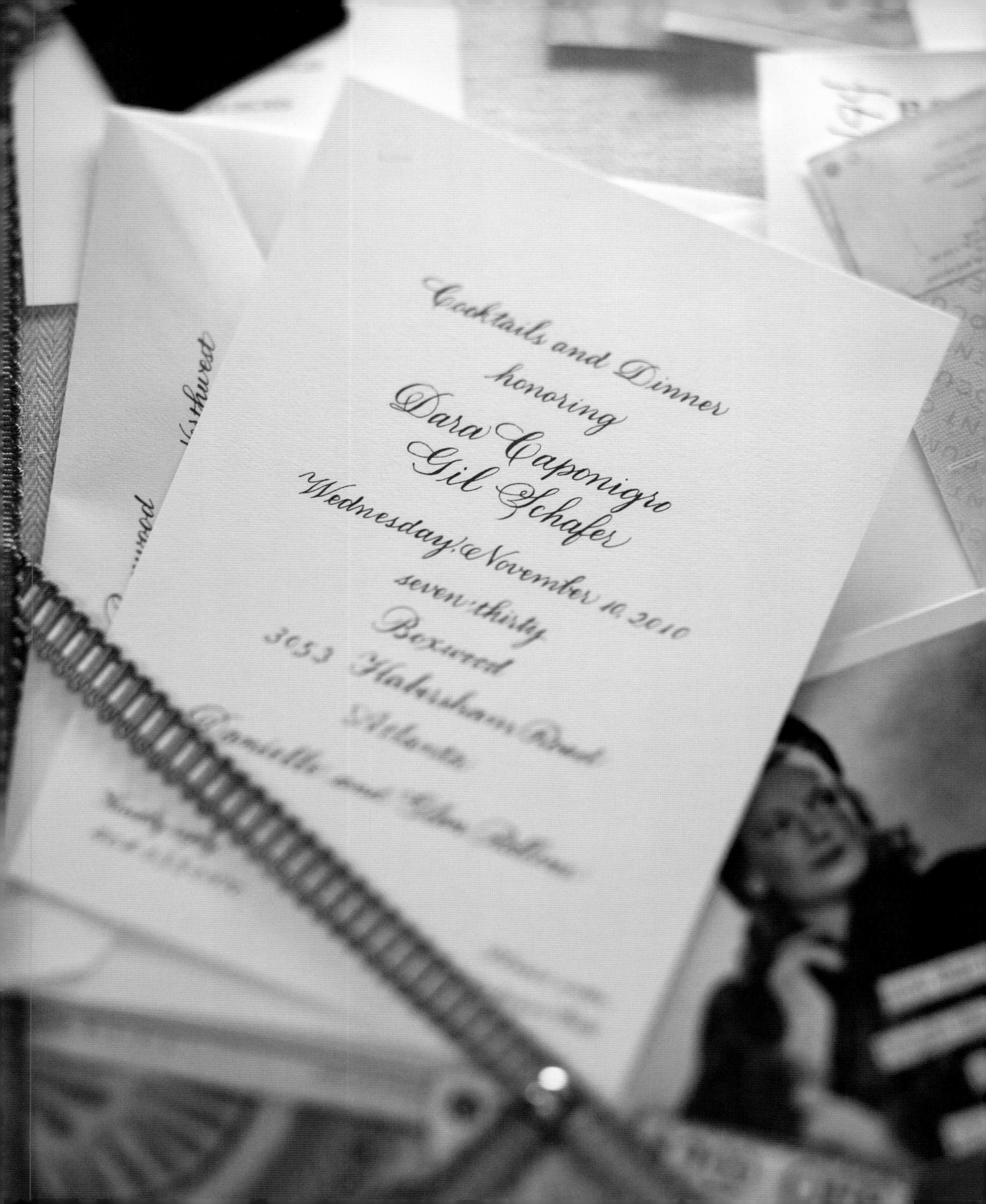

Cocktails and Dinner
honoring
Dara Caponigro
Gil Schafer
Wednesday, November 10 2010
seven-thirty
Boxwood
3053 Habersham Road
Atlanta

Weather in late fall can be unpredictable, so while I waited until the last minute to decide if the event would take place inside or out, I carefully planned every other detail. Before any party, I do a military-general-style walk-through, from a guest's vantage point. I start with their entrance, finish with their exit, and I hit everything in between. The week before this event, I mapped out table configurations using newspaper cutouts to scale, and I tried a few different options. It's best to stare down logistical issues in advance, like ensuring the caterers will have enough room to circulate. It's certainly easier to prevent a catastrophe than to correct one mid-party.

Once Mother Nature gave the thumbs-up, I used several small tables to create two long, narrow tables covered with table cloths made from fabric leftover from a decorating project. Two dramatically lit dwarf Japanese lace leaf maples created a sculptural focal point, taking full advantage of what nature provided for a backdrop. My favorite caterer, Dennis Dean, used my own recipes to craft a menu of delicious comfort food. It was practically a home-cooked meal, and I could rest easy knowing it was a guaranteed crowd pleaser. Dessert was delicious: individual fried apple pies from Holeman & Finch Bread Co., served hot with cinnamon ice cream and warm cinnamon sauce. Artisanal Bourbon Brown Derby cocktails, served in heavy, double old-fashioned orange tumblers, were flowing both for cocktail hour and after dinner as guests retreated to the living room to warm up by the Adams carved-mantel fireplace.

Entertaining should start the moment someone walks in the front door. A crisply lit and clean front door says welcome. Small details such as fresh flowers and warm lighting are always inviting.

When entertaining, keeping in mind my guests' comfort is key. Thoughtful details such as standing heaters placed near the tables and piles of blankets passed by servers kept everyone warm and toasty.

CHAMOMILE-THYME BROWN DERBY

12 ounces Chamomile and Thyme Honey
 Simple Syrup (see recipe below)
16 ounces Bulleit Bourbon
16 ounces freshly squeezed ruby red grapefruit juice,
 readily available in most supermarkets
 (or 3 to 4 medium grapefruit)
Freshly squeezed lemon juice, enough for
 a dash in each glass
8 lemon wedges
Ice, enough for 8 glasses
8 double old-fashioned glasses

1. To make the Chamomile and Thyme Honey Simple Syrup, combine equal parts honey and water in a saucepan (about 2 cups each); add a chamomile tea bag and 2 to 3 sprigs fresh thyme. Heat, stirring constantly, until honey dissolves. Let cool and strain into a container until ready to use. Store in an airtight container in the refrigerator for up to 2 weeks.

2. Mix the Bourbon, grapefruit juice, and Chamomile and Thyme Honey Simple Syrup in a pitcher.

3. To serve individual drinks, add ice to double old-fashioned glasses and fill with the Brown Derby mix. Squeeze in a dash of lemon juice, then garnish with a slice of lemon and a sprig of thyme.

Taste and adjust seasoning; add a pinch of nutmeg. Serve immediately or chill, stored in an airtight container.

3. To serve, pour hot soup into demitasse cups, shot glasses, or egg cups with a breadstick placed across the top.

BREADSTICKS
1 package puff pastry
2 tablespoons olive oil
½ cup grated Parmesan cheese
Sea salt to taste

1. Preheat oven to 375°F.

2. Cut puff pastry into small strips about ½ inch wide. Arrange on a baking sheet. Brush with oil and sprinkle with Parmesan and salt. Bake 5 to 7 minutes or until golden brown.

ENDIVE SALAD WITH LEMON VINAIGRETTE

2 heads Belgian endive
3 oranges
1 bunch fresh assorted herbs, such as fennel fronds, dill, chive tips, lemon verbena, tarragon, and parsley
Sea salt and freshly ground black pepper

LEMON VINAIGRETTE
2 tablespoons Champagne vinegar
6 tablespoons freshly squeezed lemon juice (about 2 lemons)
½ shallot, minced
½ teaspoon Dijon mustard
1 cup grapeseed oil
Sea salt and freshly ground black pepper

1. Cut each endive in half and remove core. Cut into thin slices. Peel orange with a knife and segment it by cutting in between the white pith, keeping the shapes as round as possible, making sure that all the pith has been cut away.

2. To make the vinaigrette put vinegar, lemon juice, shallot, and mustard in a blender or food processor. Blend on high about 30 seconds then slowly pour in oil and mix on high 1 to 2 minutes.

3. Wash and dry herbs. Place all salad ingredients in a large bowl, toss with lemon vinaigrette, and season with salt and pepper to taste.

BUTTERNUT SQUASH SOUP SHOOTERS

2 small butternut squash (about 4 pounds total)
5 tablespoons unsalted butter
Sea salt and freshly ground black pepper
6 cups chicken stock
Pinch of nutmeg
Breadsticks (see recipe below)

1. Preheat oven to 375°F. Cut squashes in half lengthwise. Remove seeds and divide 1 tablespoon butter, cubed, among the cavities. Season with salt and pepper to taste. Place flesh side up in a roasting pan and cook until tender, about 25 minutes. Remove from oven and let cool.

2. Heat stock in a saucepan over medium heat. When squash is slightly cooled, peel. Place one quarter of the roasted squash in a blender and add a quarter of the stock. Puree 20 seconds or until very smooth. Add 1 tablespoon butter and blend. Pour the mixture into a large container and repeat process with the remaining squash three more times until all of the squash is pureed.

ROAST CHICKEN WITH RISOTTO AND MUSHROOM FRICASSEE

2 tablespoons extra-virgin olive oil
8 chicken breasts, skin on, preferably free-range
Sea salt and freshly ground black pepper
1 tablespoon unsalted butter
3 thyme sprigs
1 parsley sprig
1 clove garlic, crushed
Risotto (see recipe below)
Mushroom Fricassee (see recipe below)

1. Preheat oven to 375°F.

2. Heat oil in a large ovenproof skillet. Rinse and pat chicken dry. Season with salt and pepper to taste.

3. When oil starts to shimmer, add chicken, skin side down, making sure not to overcrowd the pan. Sear until skin is brown and crisp. Flip chicken and place the pan in oven. Roast, basting chicken every 10 minutes with the juices, until the thickest part of meat registers 160°F.

4. When chicken is done, place the pan on the stovetop over medium heat. Add butter, thyme, parsley, and garlic. Baste again, for about 1 minute. This will impart the flavor of the herbs to the chicken and make it extra juicy. Let chicken rest 4 minutes after basting.

5. To serve, place a helping of risotto on each plate, a little off center. Lay a chicken breast on top of each helping of risotto, overlapping it slightly, then spoon mushroom fricassee on top of the chicken and serve immediately.

RISOTTO
2 quarts chicken stock
6 tablespoons unsalted butter
3 tablespoons olive oil
4 shallots, minced
3 celery ribs, minced
3 cups Arborio rice
1 cup dry white wine
1 cup grated Parmesan cheese
¾ cup heavy cream
Sea salt and freshly ground black pepper

1. Heat stock in a saucepan, bring to a boil, then reduce heat to low.

2. Heat 4 tablespoons butter and oil in a large pan and sauté shallots and celery over medium heat until tender. Add rice and coat thoroughly with butter and oil. Stir frequently but allow the grains of rice to toast. After about 2 minutes, deglaze the pan with wine.

3. Let wine reduce until evaporated, then start ladling in hot stock a few ladlefuls at a time. Allow rice to absorb each ladle of stock before adding more. Stir with a wooden spoon every minute or so and make sure that no rice sticks to bottom of pan. Repeat until all liquid is absorbed and rice is cooked but al dente, about 14 minutes.

4. Finish risotto by stirring in remaining butter, Parmesan, and cream. Season with salt and pepper to taste.

MUSHROOM FRICASSEE
1 pound fresh wild mushrooms, such as morel, shiitake, or chanterelle
½ cup unsalted butter
¼ cup all-purpose flour
2 tablespoons olive oil
3 shallots, sliced
½ cup dry white wine
3 cups organic chicken broth
1 bay leaf
2 sprigs fresh thyme
1 sprig parsley
Dash of Cognac
Sea salt and freshly ground black pepper

1. Remove stems and any dirt from mushrooms, using a damp cloth; cut into large pieces. Melt ¼ cup butter with flour in a medium-size saucepan over low heat, stirring occasionally for about 10 minutes and making sure that the roux does not brown. Reserve.

2. Heat oil with remaining ¼ cup butter over medium-high heat. Add mushrooms, being careful not to crowd the pan, and sauté; you may have to do this in several batches. Avoid stirring too frequently in order to allow mushrooms to brown. Add shallot and reduce heat to medium. Cook until shallots are translucent; deglaze pan with wine then let alcohol evaporate, about 2 minutes. Add broth and roux and stir.

3. Tie bay leaf, thyme, and parsley together with kitchen string and add to mushrooms. Let cook until stock is reduced by half. Add Cognac and season with salt and pepper to taste. Cool in an ice bath and refrigerate, or keep warm if using immediately.

BROWN SUGAR–SAUTÉED RAINBOW CARROTS

1 pound baby
  rainbow carrots
2 tablespoons
  unsalted butter
1 tablespoon extra-virgin
  olive oil
2 tablespoons brown sugar
¼ cup chopped fresh parsley

1. Clean and peel carrots, leaving ¼ inch green leafy tops. Use a paring knife to clean any dirt away from where the carrot meets the greens. Parboil carrots in boiling water 5 minutes, or just until they start to soften.

2. Heat butter and oil in a large pan and sauté carrots 2 minutes. Sprinkle with brown sugar and cook another minute. Garnish with parsley.

HOLEMAN & FINCH FRIED APPLE PIES WITH CINNAMON ICE CREAM

This recipe was inspired by the wonderful fried pies served at Holeman & Finch, a favorite gastropub and watering hole in Atlanta known for their late-night snacks. Cinnamon ice cream is the best topping. Use ½ gallon of your favorite store-bought vanilla ice cream. Let it soften a bit (you don't want it completely melted), place in the bowl of a standing mixer with the paddle attachment, and gently fold in 4 to 6 teaspoons ground cinnamon. Refreeze and serve on top of the hot apple pies. Time-saving tip: These pies can be prepared, but not baked, and placed in the freezer until you are ready to use them, up to a month in advance. Then on party day, pull them out of the freezer and bake them while you're eating dinner.

TART DOUGH

3¾ cups bread flour
Pinch of sea salt
12 tablespoons cold
  unsalted butter
1 large egg
6 tablespoons cold water
Dash of white vinegar
Flour (for dusting)
½ cup melted butter
  (for brushing pies
  before baking)
Cinnamon sugar or
  powdered sugar glaze
  (see recipe below)

APPLE FILLING

1 pound apples such as Golden Delicious, Granny Smith,
  or Fuji, diced
3½ tablespoons sugar
Pinch each of salt, ground allspice, ground cardamom, ground
  cinnamon, ground cloves, ground ginger, ground nutmeg
Dash of vanilla extract
2 tablespoons cornstarch

TOPPINGS

CINNAMON SUGAR:	POWDERED SUGAR GLAZE:
½ cup sugar	½ cup powdered sugar
1 tablespoon cinnamon	2 tablespoons warm water
Blend.	Whisk to combine.

1. To make tart dough, combine flour and salt in the bowl of a stand mixer with paddle attachment. Add butter and mix until a coarse meal forms.

2. Combine egg, water, and vinegar in another bowl. Add wet ingredients to dry ones, mixing only until the dough comes together, adding more cold water as needed. Roll the dough into a disk, wrap in plastic, and refrigerate until ready to use, at least 30 minutes.

3. To make apple filling, place apples in a large pot over medium-low heat. Add all remaining ingredients except cornstarch. Stir well to combine and cook until apples begin to soften. Remove from heat.

4. Strain all liquid from apples into another container, reserving apples. Pour the liquid back into the pot and warm the liquid over medium heat.

5. Combine cornstarch and 2 tablespoons cold water into a slurry, or thin paste. Once the liquid on the stove has warmed, slowly add the slurry, stirring continuously until smooth.

6. Remove the sauce from the heat and allow it to cool completely. Once cooled, add back to the apples and stir to thoroughly incorporate. Refrigerate until chilled.

7. To prepare tarts, roll out dough on a lightly floured surface to ⅛ inch thick. Mold dough into 6-inch flat rounds. Fill the tart rounds with 1 tablespoon of the apple filling. Crimp the edges of the tarts, using the tines of a fork. Freeze until ready to bake.

8. When ready to bake, preheat oven to 325°F.

9. Brush both sides of each tart with melted butter. Bake 20 to 25 minutes on a rimmed cookie sheet; bake 7 to 10 minutes longer if the pies are frozen.

10. Serve hot, sprinkling each tart liberally with the cinnamon-sugar or the powdered sugar glaze.

A HOLIDAY CELEBRATION OF FRIENDSHIP

Serves 8

Rosé Champagne with Pomegranate Seeds

Vanilla Bean Champagne **

Grilled Cheese with Crème Fraîche,
Caviar, and Smoked Salmon

Mushroom-Filled Beggars' Purses

Potatoes with Crème Fraîche and Caviar

Endive Salad with Roasted Beets, Blue Cheese,
and Honey-Sherry Vinaigrette **

Roasted Beef Tenderloin with Rosemary and Garlic**

Mashed Potatoes

Sautéed Haricots Verts with Hazelnuts

Sticky Toffee Pudding
with Cinnamon Whipped Cream **

I'M DREAMING OF A BLONDE CHRISTMAS

The five of us have been the closest of friends for many years. We have been together through thick and thin (literally and figuratively), highlights and lowlights, single and double processes, and even the occasional life twists that makeup cannot cover. Over the years we have decided that the best gift that we can give to one another during the hustle and bustle of the holiday season is a night off to enjoy time together. So every December we happily take turns playing hostess for our favorite Christmas tradition: a festive dinner and gift exchange.

When it was Cynthia and Brad Hammond's turn to host the dinner, their gorgeous Georgian home in Buckhead was the perfect setting. Cynthia's concept for the evening was a dinner inspired by Old World English Christmas traditions with a hint of rustic elegance. Her vision included a warm and cozy red room, yet her dining room was decidedly yellow, so with a quick change of furniture, Cynthia cleverly turned an upstairs sitting room that had walls covered in a cheery red Cowtan & Tout toile into a dining room for the night. Dinners don't always have to be in the dining room—dining elsewhere in the house can create a welcome sense of adventure and spontaneity.

A large creamware bowl heaped with ruby pomegranates sat on the sideboard, which was draped with fragrant bay garlands. Gifts from Santa, carefully wrapped in coordinating colors, were piled high on a pair of red tole-painted chairs for all who had been naughty or nice. The dining table was covered

PREVIOUS PAGES: *Invitations on thick ivory cardstock, lined with Florentine paper and written in beautiful red calligraphy, were tied with ruby-colored hand-dyed silk ribbons and hand delivered.* OPPOSITE: *With "No regrets" instead of the standard RSVP, it was obvious that this year's dinner would be a fun one.*

I'm dreaming of a
Blonde Christmas Dinner
December 17, 2010
7 o'clock pm
Woodhaven

Cynthia & Brad Hammond

No regrets   Black tie

It's important to celebrate life's little moments. A Champagne toast to friendship and best wishes for survival of the upcoming holidays started the evening on a glamorous note.

VANILLA BEAN CHAMPAGNE

8 ounces Bourbon
8 Madagascar vanilla beans
1 bottle of Champagne, chilled
8 chilled Champagne flutes or tall pilsner glasses

1. In a small saucepan bring Bourbon to a simmer. Add the vanilla beans and let simmer 10 to 15 minutes or until soft and tender.

2. Remove vanilla beans from Bourbon, shaking off the excess, and let the beans cool.

3. To serve, split beans in half lengthwise with a knife and place in Champagne flutes; top each flute with Champagne.

Bourbon-infused vanilla bean Champagne served in old-fashioned coupes added a dazzling, retro touch.

in layers of crisp ivory linen and set with glistening silver and snowy creamware. In a single, large, clear cylinder vase, richly colored peonies and sprays of pepper berry anchored by cranberries to hide the stems made the perfect centerpiece. The names on the place cards were written in scrumptious curlicues of calligraphy and, instead of our given names, our hostess had devised ingenious nicknames for each guest based on funny little shared memories accumulated over the years. We were surprised and delighted as we tried to guess which "alias" described each of us.

Champagne flavored with whole vanilla beans that had been simmered in Bourbon perfectly complemented the classic hors d'oeuvres of Grilled Cheese with Smoked Salmon and Caviar, Mushroom-Filled Beggars' Purses, and tiny fingerling potatoes stuffed with caviar and crème fraîche that were enjoyed around the Christmas tree.

After a wonderful, winter-inspired traditional Christmas dinner of beef tenderloin, delectable mashed potatoes, and haricots vert with hazelnuts, a dessert of sticky toffee pudding was served in heavy, etched crystal bowls and dolloped with cinnamon whipped cream and caramel ice cream. Making the often-requested sticky toffee pudding the night before not only allowed the flavors to meld but also removed a little bit of the pre-party stress, and I was still able to serve a homemade dessert! The evening ended with a Champagne toast on the balcony, and, even with the frosty chill in the night air, we were thoroughly warmed by our strong bond of female friendship.

The festive table was covered with a spider-hemstitched overlay on top of simple ivory linen and paired with timelessly elegant hemstitched napkins, and set with creamware. Intricate, antique Tiffany Persian silver settings from 1868 (a hundred years older than the hostess herself) were mixed with mother-of-pearl handled dinner knives from J. Russell. Inexpensive red water glasses added a cheery touch to the snowy white table.

ABOVE: *A loose arrangement of peonies, pepper berries, and roses, anchored by cranberries and placed in a simple glass container, created a perfect holiday centerpiece.* OPPOSITE: *Following dinner, a festive gift exchange in which each woman had four of the same gift elaborately wrapped for the other women (and their partners did the same) made for a madcap, laughter-filled visit from Santa!*

ENDIVE SALAD WITH ROASTED BEETS, BLUE CHEESE, AND HONEY-SHERRY VINAIGRETTE

HONEY-SHERRY VINAIGRETTE
¼ cup sherry vinegar
2 tablespoons honey
1 cup grapeseed oil
Sea salt and freshly ground black pepper

SALAD
2 small beets, 1 red and 1 golden
1 teaspoon olive oil
2 heads green Belgian endive
2 heads red Belgian endive
3 large blood oranges
½ cup blue cheese, crumbled (optional, for garnish)
½ cup toasted hazelnuts, chopped (optional, for garnish)
Salt and freshly ground black pepper

1. Make the vinaigrette by combining vinegar and honey in a small bowl. Whisk in oil and season with salt and pepper to taste. Set aside.

2. Preheat oven to 350°F. Wash beets and pierce all over with a fork. Rub with a little bit of oil and wrap in foil. Bake about 20 minutes or until tender when pierced with a knife. Let cool.

3. Core endive and wash leaves; pat dry. Segment oranges by cutting off the tops and bottoms of the oranges and then cutting off the skin. Remove segments using a sharp knife, being careful to cut away the white pith. Peel beets and dice.

4. Combine endive and oranges in a large bowl and toss with vinaigrette. Season with salt and pepper to taste.

5. To serve, divide among plates and garnish with cheese and hazelnuts, if desired.

ROASTED BEEF TENDERLOIN
WITH ROSEMARY AND GARLIC

1½ tablespoons sea salt
2 to 3 tablespoons coarsely cracked black peppercorns
2 tablespoons chopped fresh rosemary
2 cloves garlic, minced
4 tablespoons olive oil
1 (4- to 5-pound) center-cut beef tenderloin roast,
  trimmed and tied

SAUCE
2 tablespoons unsalted butter
½ cup shallots, chopped
2 cloves garlic, chopped
1 fresh rosemary sprig
1 tablespoon Dijon mustard
1 cup Port

2 cups beef stock, preferably homemade
  (or store-bought low-sodium stock)
2 to 3 tablespoons crème fraîche

GARNISH
Fresh pomegranate halves
Fresh rosemary sprigs

1. Combine salt, peppercorns, rosemary, and garlic
   together in a small bowl. Add 2 tablespoons oil and stir.
   Rub paste all over beef. Let sit at room temperature
   1 hour before roasting.

2. To make sauce, melt the butter in a medium-size saucepan
   over medium heat. Add shallots and sauté until soft, about
   3 minutes. Add garlic, rosemary, and mustard and stir. Add
   Port and stock. Cook until reduced to about 1½ cups and
   thick, about 20 minutes. Strain liquid mixture into a fine-

mesh sieve over a bowl, pressing on the solids to extract as much liquid as possible. Discard solids and reserve sauce.

3. Position rack in center of oven and preheat to 425°F.

4. Heat remaining 2 tablespoons oil in a large skillet over high heat. Pat meat dry with a paper towel so it will brown nicely. Sear beef on all sides, 5 to 7 minutes total. Place beef in roasting pan and roast until an instant-read thermometer inserted into the thickest part of meat registers 125°F for medium-rare (135°F to 140°F in thinnest part), 20 to 25 minutes. Remove roast from oven; tent lightly with foil and let rest 10 minutes.

5. Bring sauce to a boil and whisk in crème fraîche; reduce heat to low and cook another minute. Adjust seasoning and serve warm.

6. Cut string from roast. Cut roast crosswise into ½-inch-thick slices and arrange on warm platter. Serve with sauce and garnish, if desired.

STICKY TOFFEE PUDDING WITH CINNAMON WHIPPED CREAM

2½ teaspoons baking powder
Pinch of sea salt
1 cup pitted Medjool dates, chopped,
   plus 8 whole dates for garnish
¾ cup unsalted butter, softened
¾ cup brown sugar
1 teaspoon vanilla extract, or 1 vanilla bean, halved
1 large egg, lightly beaten
1 cup all-purpose flour, plus more for pan
Sticky Toffee Sauce (see recipe below)
Cinnamon Whipped Cream (see recipe below)

1. Preheat oven to 350°F.

2. Bring 1 cup water to a boil in a small saucepan. Add 1 teaspoon baking powder, salt, and chopped dates. Remove from heat and let steep 30 minutes. Drain and reserve dates.

3. Butter and flour a 9-inch square cake pan. Cream butter and brown sugar in bowl of a stand mixer on medium speed about 2½ minutes. Add vanilla (scrape the bean, if using) and egg.

4. Sift flour and the remaining 1½ teaspoons baking powder together; fold in dates. Add the flour mixture to the butter mixture; reduce mixing speed to low and mix until smooth. Pour batter into the cake pan and bake until the top is springy and a tester inserted in the center comes out clean, about 30 minutes.

5. Place cake in pan on a cooling rack. Poke holes at 1-inch intervals all over the cake using a chopstick. Pour half of Sticky Toffee Sauce over the cake and let it rest about 20 minutes. The cake can be stored up to 1 day in a sealed container in the refrigerator and reheated just before serving in a 350°F oven about 20 minutes, adding more sauce if it seems too dry.

6. To serve, slice the cake into squares, heat the remaining sauce, and heavily drizzle it over each slice, topping with Cinnamon Whipped Cream and garnishing with a whole date.

STICKY TOFFEE SAUCE
½ cup unsalted butter
½ cup heavy cream
1 cup brown sugar

1. Combine all ingredients in a saucepan and bring to a boil.

2. Whisk to incorporate. Reduce heat to low, continuing to whisk until mixture is thickened, about 5 minutes.

CINNAMON WHIPPED CREAM
1 cup heavy cream
3 tablespoons powdered sugar
1 teaspoon ground cinnamon

1. Combine all ingredients in a chilled metal bowl and beat (with a standing mixer, hand-held mixer, or by hand) until thickened but not stiff. Do not over-whip.

2. Chill, covered, until ready to serve.

Keeping a holiday dinner on the traditional side helps get everyone in the spirit. Warm, comforting food is always delectable!

AN ELEGANT NEW YEAR'S EVE DINNER

Serves 8

VODKA BAR

FRENCH 75 **

CAVIAR AND BLINIS

SWEDISH GRAVLAX SALAD ON TOAST **

KUMAMOTO OYSTERS WITH
LEMON MOUSSE AND HORSERADISH **

ESCAROLE SALAD WITH PICKLED ONIONS
AND BLOOD ORANGES **

SAUTÉED GULF SNAPPER WITH CARDAMOM HONEY
AND SPAGHETTI SQUASH

SHORT RIBS WITH TURNIP GREENS, FARRO,
AND BOILED PEANUTS **

CHOCOLATE MOUSSE WITH ESPRESSO ICE CREAM **

A SILVER AND GOLD CELEBRATION

White boxes holding a silver-plated noisemaker nestled in tinsel and a sumptuous handwritten invitation tied up in sterling French wired ribbon summoned a very small group of close friends to a sparkling New Year's Eve dinner. The dress code specified shimmering metallics: gold and silver for the ladies and black tie for the gentlemen. Robin and Hilton Howell, gracious bon vivants who have never met a stranger, relish any opportunity to entertain. New Year's Eve is a perfect time for hosting

PREVIOUS PAGE: *A Vermeil Francis I pitcher holds French 75s, a Champagne cocktail, to start the evening out right.* ABOVE: *The dress code specified shimmering metallics: gold and silver for the ladies and black tie for the gentlemen. Robin and Hilton Howell, gracious bon vivants who have never met a stranger, relish any opportunity to entertain.* OPPOSITE PAGE: *As the clock struck midnight, the Champagne cork was popped and everyone lifted a glass to ring in the New Year with a little sparkle.*

intimate friends at home, and I spent the day with them preparing for a festive dinner to bid adieu to the old year and ring in the new.

An elegant cocktail hour featured French 75s along with vintage Champagnes served from the "Preacher's Bar," an armoire opened to reveal a hidden bar from which drinks are served. Spicy, cold vodka, frozen in blocks of ice with pretty flowers and berries and set on silver trays with stacks of silver shot glasses, added a stunning visual for a vodka tasting. Set up on a table in the living room, the tasting not only provided entertainment but also complemented the briny taste of the caviar in crystal servers with blinis and crème fraîche. Noted Atlanta chef and great friend Shaun Doty prepared a spectacular formal menu. One favorite appetizer that had guests waiting in the kitchen were tiny fried quail eggs placed atop a gravlax salad on toast—something absolutely decadent yet unbelievably simple and easy to prepare.

Table settings are a special hallmark of the Howells' parties, as they are always pulling from their well-curated and ever-growing collections of china, crystal, and silver—the perfect blend of inherited family heirlooms mixed with flea market finds from treasure expeditions as far afield as the *marchés aux puces* in Paris to the local Scott Antique Markets in Atlanta. Guest place settings were marked with silver seashells, a reference to good luck, bearing silver-covered chocolates and place cards with names written in beautiful calligraphy. The dining room was softly lit with candlelight and the table was lavishly set to capture the sparkle of the evening. Arrangements of white roses and pineapples, a symbol of welcome and hospitality held over from precolonial days' traditions, sat in the center of the table and on the sideboard. As the hours waned, dinnertime conversation turned to resolutions and celebratory Champagne toasting over a dessert of rich chocolate mousse with espresso ice cream and whipped cream with chocolate shavings. The golden night concluded with a midnight countdown and a festive welcoming of the New Year with our silver noisemakers in hand, watching the ball drop in Times Square with the sound muted on the television.

White roses arranged tightly in a low centerpiece complement the silver, vermeil, and glassware. Antique Italian Murano stems are paired with American cut glass wineglasses and Wedgwood sterling water goblets. Antique French sterling and crystal decanters and open salt and pepper cellars add to the splendor of the table. All these beautiful pieces, collected over many years, and in some cases generations, help create the dramatic beauty of the New Year's celebration.

White boxes holding a silver-plated noisemaker nestled in tinsel and a sumptuous handwritten invitation
tied up in sterling French wired ribbon summoned a very small group of close friends to a sparkling
New Year's Eve dinner. OPPOSITE PAGE: A selection of fine Champagnes stands ready for the
night's festivities beneath a majestic yet simple arrangement of lilies and ilex berries in the Howells' foyer.

FRENCH 75

12 ounces Boodles British gin
8 ounces lemon simple syrup (see recipe below)
8 ounces freshly squeezed lemon juice (8 to 10 lemons)
1 bottle Champagne, chilled
8 chilled Champagne coupes filled with crushed ice

In a large pitcher, combine gin, simple syrup, and lemon juice and stir. Fill chilled Champagne glasses with crushed ice and fill the glasses about one third of the way with the gin lemonade. Top each glass with about 2 ounces Champagne just before serving.

LEMON SIMPLE SYRUP

1 cup sugar
Zest of 2 to 3 lemons
Juice of 1 lemon

Combine 1 cup water and sugar in a saucepan. Bring to a boil, stirring constantly until sugar dissolves and the liquid becomes clear. Reduce heat and simmer, stirring continuously, 5 to 10 minutes. Remove from heat and let cool to room temperature. Add lemon zest and juice. Pour into a container. Syrup will keep in the refrigerator for up to 2 weeks.

"Life is enriched beyond measure when we are with the ones we love, as our memories are never more vivid than when we are with our beloved family and friends. Let us raise a glass to the memories of last year, and for the ones of tomorrow." —C. Michael Gibson

Submerge a full bottle of vodka or other alcohol into a fully opened cardboard milk or juice carton filled partially with water. Add flowers, herbs, or thinly sliced fruit to the water and place the carton upright in the freezer until the water is frozen. Repeat the process; doing it in stages allows the contents to freeze floating in the water rather than sinking to the bottom. When the liquid is completely frozen, take the carton from the freezer and remove the carton from the ice block by cutting the sides of the box open. Display liquor on a tray lined with folded cloths to catch drips as the ice thaws. After using, simply reinsert the bottle and any remaining ice block into another carton, add water, and refreeze! This is simple elegance that requires only a minimum of effort. If you keep one in the freezer, you're prepared for any last-minute party! Note: This method will work with any alcohol: it's perfect for tequila frozen in water with sliced limes, gin with cucumber slices or, to add zing to a Bloody Mary bar—vodka suspended in an ice block with pepper berries or olives!

1. Place regular eggs in a medium pot and add enough cold water to cover. Turn heat to high and when water comes to a boil, turn off heat, cover the pot, and let the eggs sit 12 minutes. Remove eggs and shock in an ice bath. Peel eggs, rinsing gently to remove their shells, then chop very finely and put in a large mixing bowl. Add gravlax, mayonnaise, lemon juice, dill, and Maldon salt and pepper to taste. Mix gently. Refrigerate the salad while making toasts or until ready to serve.

2. Preheat oven to 375°F. Cut baguette into ⅛-inch slices, approximately 30 slices. Place slices on a baking sheet and brush with oil then sprinkle with salt. Toast until just crisp and golden, about 8 minutes per side.

3. To serve, gently heat butter and about 1 teaspoon of oil over low heat in a nonstick pan. When butter begins to sizzle, turn off heat and crack quail eggs carefully into the pan to barely cook sunny side up just until the whites are set but the yolk remains uncooked. Repeat as necessary to cook all eggs. Divide the gravlax salad evenly on the pieces of toast; garnish each with a fried quail egg, and serve immediately.

KUMAMOTO OYSTERS WITH LEMON MOUSSE AND HORSERADISH

6 large egg whites
6 tablespoons lemon juice (about 2 lemons)
Sea salt
¼ cup grapeseed oil
24 shucked Kumamoto oysters, on the half shell
Crushed ice, enough to spread as a bed for oysters on 8 plates
¼ cup grated fresh horseradish
2 tablespoons minced chives (for garnish)

1. Combine egg whites and lemon juice in a blender. Add a pinch of salt and blend, then, with blender running, slowly add a steady stream of oil. Remove mousse from the blender and chill until ready to use in a covered bowl, but no more than 2 hours.

2. To serve, divide the crushed ice among 8 plates and place 3 oysters on each plate. Top each oyster with a teaspoon of lemon mousse and a teaspoon of horseradish. Garnish with chives and serve immediately.

SWEDISH GRAVLAX SALAD ON TOAST

Gravlax is a Swedish-style raw salmon cured in sugar and salt. You can find it at gourmet food shops or online. I especially like www.russanddaughters.com.

3 large eggs
1½ pounds Swedish gravlax, chopped
1 cup mayonnaise
6 tablespoons freshly squeezed lemon juice (about 2 lemons)
1 tablespoon chopped fresh dill
Maldon salt and freshly ground black pepper
1 baguette
½ cup extra-virgin olive oil
1 tablespoon unsalted butter
8 to 10 fresh quail eggs

ABOVE: *Chef Shaun Doty at work.*

ESCAROLE SALAD WITH PICKLED ONIONS AND BLOOD ORANGES

2 cups freshly squeezed orange juice (6 to 8 oranges)
¼ cup extra-virgin olive oil
Sea salt
½ cup cider vinegar
½ cup sugar
2 cups thinly sliced red onions
4 heads escarole
8 blood oranges
¼ cup aged balsamic vinegar

1. Heat orange juice in a small saucepan over medium-high heat and cook until reduced by half, then chill. Place chilled orange juice in a blender, slowly adding the oil in a steady stream to emulsify. Season with salt to taste and set dressing aside.

2. Bring cider vinegar, sugar, and a pinch of salt to boil in a small saucepan; pour over sliced onions. Chill.

3. To serve, wash and dry escarole. Peel oranges with a knife, cut off both ends and slice. Place escarole and half the blood oranges in a bowl, add dressing and a pinch of salt, and toss well to combine. Divide salad evenly among 8 chilled plates and garnish with pickled onions and remaining orange slices. Drizzle each salad with balsamic vinegar and serve immediately.

SHORT RIBS WITH TURNIP GREENS, FARRO, AND BOILED PEANUTS

¾ cup unsalted butter
¼ cup extra-virgin olive oil
8 pounds bone-in short ribs
Sea salt and freshly ground black pepper
3 onions
1 bunch celery
4 carrots
12 cloves garlic, finely chopped
4 (750-ml) bottles Malbec wine
2 (14.5-ounce) cans whole peeled Italian tomatoes

1 bay leaf
Farro (see recipe below)
Turnip Greens (see recipe below)
Boiled Peanuts (see recipe below)

1. Preheat oven to 200°F. Heat butter and oil in a large roasting pan over medium-high heat until butter melts and oil shimmers. Season ribs with salt and pepper to taste, then sear on both sides until brown, about 10 minutes. Add onions, celery, carrots, and garlic and cook, stirring occasionally, until tender and caramelized. Add wine, tomatoes, and bay leaf and bring to a boil. Add a big pinch of salt and a couple twists of ground pepper. Wrap the pan tightly with aluminum foil or cover with a lid and place the pan on the center rack of the oven. Cook 10 hours, or until tender.

2. Gently remove ribs from the pan and cool. Strain and reduce the remaining liquid in the pan to about 8 cups total and skim the excess fat. Reserve the liquid for basting the ribs when you reheat them. When ribs are cool enough to handle, tidy them a bit by removing the excess fat and connective tissue and portion into 8 servings, using a knife to cut. Wrap individually in plastic wrap and chill.

3. To reheat, preheat oven to 200°F, unwrap ribs, and place them in a roasting pan with the reserved liquid. Cover the pan and place it in the oven for 1 hour.

4. To serve, remove ribs and baste to glaze them. Divide the farro among serving plates and top each with a short rib. Spoon peanuts over each rib and garnish with sea salt. Add turnip greens. Serve immediately.

FARRO
6 tablespoons unsalted butter
4 cups farro
Sprig of thyme
Sea salt and freshly ground black pepper

Bring 2½ quarts water to a boil; add butter, farro, thyme, and salt and pepper to taste. Reduce heat to low; simmer until tender, about 20 minutes. Reserve warm.

TURNIP GREENS
2 bunches turnip greens, chopped
6 tablespoons unsalted butter
2 shallots, thinly sliced
½ cup chicken stock
Sea salt and freshly ground black pepper

1. Wash and dry turnip greens, remove the stems, and chop greens about 1 inch wide.

2. Heat butter in a pan over medium heat. Add shallots and cook until tender, about 1½ minutes. Add turnip greens and stock and sauté until tender, about 5 minutes. Season with salt and pepper to taste. Reserve warm.

BOILED PEANUTS
2 pounds raw, or "green," peanuts in shell
¼ cup Creole seasoning
Sea salt

Wash and place peanuts in a large pot and cover with 2 gallons water. Add Creole seasoning and two big pinches of salt. Bring to a boil and simmer 4 to 5 hours, adding more water as necessary, until tender when peeled. Drain peanuts, reserving 1 cup of the liquid. When peanuts are cool enough to handle, peel shells and add peanuts to reserved liquid. Keep warm.

CHOCOLATE MOUSSE WITH ESPRESSO ICE CREAM

2 (9.7-ounce) dark chocolate bars, preferably Scharffen Berger, Valrhona, or other good-quality European-style chocolate, 1 bar for melting and 1 bar, grated, for garnish
1½ cups heavy cream
2 large eggs, lightly beaten
3 large egg yolks
½ cup sugar
Pinch of salt
Espresso Ice Cream (see recipe below)
Cacao nibs (for garnish, preferably Scharffen Berger)
8 wineglasses

1. Place 1 dark chocolate bar (broken into pieces) in top pan of a double boiler and continuously stir over low heat until the chocolate has fully melted. Remove from heat and let stand.

2. In a separate bowl, beat cream with a whisk until it holds stiff peaks. In another small bowl, whisk eggs and yolks together, add sugar and salt, and whisk until foamy. Add a spatula full of chocolate to egg mixture and fold in, then add all the egg mixture to the chocolate and blend until just combined. Add a spatula full of the chocolate mixture to the cream and gently fold in, barely mixing. Add the whipped cream to the chocolate and mix until just blended. (This is called the liaison technique, which allows the mixture to slowly adjust to new ingredients without curdling.)

3. Divide evenly among 8 wineglasses and cover each with plastic wrap. Chill at least 5 hours. For best results, chill overnight.

4. To serve, scoop a portion of Espresso Ice Cream into each glass of mousse. Shave remaining chocolate bar with a grater over ice cream and add cacao nibs. Serve immediately.

ESPRESSO ICE CREAM
2 quarts organic vanilla ice cream, softened
6 tablespoons ground espresso beans

Place softened ice cream in bowl of a standing mixer and add espresso. Mix with the paddle attachment until blended. Return to freezer until ready to serve.

RESOURCES

BAKERIES & CAFÉS

Baker's Man, Inc. (koi cakes)
www.bakersmaninc.com

Café Lapin (coconut cakes)
www.cafelapin.com

H&F Bread Co.
404-350-8877
www.hfbreadco.com

Highland Bakery
www.highlandbakery.com

Sophie's Uptown
www.sophiesuptown.com

Star Provisions (bakery/restaurant/
gourmet shop)
www.starprovisions.com

CANDLES

Cire Trudon Candles
www.ciretrudon.com

Jo Malone
www.jomalone.com

Diptyque Paris
www.diptyqueparis.com

CHINA, DINNERWARE, CRYSTAL, & GLASSWARE

Deruta of Italy (Giardino)
www.artistica.com
www.contemporary concepts.com

Anthropologie
www.anthropologie.com

Baccarat
www.baccarat.com

Chef Tools (La Rochere)
www.cheftools.com

China Royale (Hermes Siesta Island)
www.chinaroyale.com

Christian Dior
www.dior.com

Gracious Style
(Reynaud Serenite Blue)
www.graciousstyle.com

Herend
www.herendstore.com

Lenox (red water glasses; Marchesa)
www.lenox.com

Michael C. Fina
www.michaelcfina.com

Mottahedeh
(Turkish Garden tin plates)
www.mottahedeh.com

Overstock
www.overstock.com

Pickard China Company (Elsie)
www.pickardchina.com

Replacements (Bernardaud Limoges
Vannerie; creamware)
www.replacements.com

Riedel (wine glasses)
www.glassware.riedel.com

Scott Antique Markets
www.scottantiquemarket.com

Star of Morocco
(multicolored Moroccan tea glasses)
www.moroccan-furniture-decor.com

Waterford (crystal)
na.wwrd.com

William Yeoward (cake dishes)
www.williamyeowardcrystal.com

DESIGNERS

Lela Rose
www.lelarose.com

Rachel Roy
www.rachelroy.com

FLATWARE

Siècle Paris
(bamboo-handled-flatware)
www.siecle-paris.com

Tiffany & Co. (Audubon silver)
www.tiffany.com

FLOWERS

Cut Flower Wholesale, Inc.
(trade only)
888-99-STEMS
www.cutflower.com

Fischer & Page (trade only)
212-645-4106

Michal Evans (floral design)
www.michalevans.com

FOOD, FOOD SHOPS & SUPPLIES

Beanilla (Madagascar vanilla beans)
www.beanilla.com

Benton's Smoky Mountain
   Country Hams
www.bentonscountryhams2.com

Byrd's Famous Cookies
(benne wafers)
www.byrdcookiecompany.com

Fancy Flours (red-and-white-
checked waxed paper)
www.fancyflours.com

Gilt Taste
www.gilttaste.com

Harney & Sons (fine teas)
www.harney.com

Karlsburger Food, Inc. (veal stock)
www.karlsburger.com

King of Pops (specialty popsicles)
www.kingofpops.net

Le Bon Marché La Grand
   Épicerie in Paris
www.lagrandeepicerie.fr

MacarOn Café (macarons)
www.macaroncafe.com

Maldon Salt Company
(finishing sea salt)
www.saltworks.us

Marx Foods (molded sorbets
and edible flowers)
www.marxfoods.com

Medjool Dates
www.medjooldates.com

Michaels (edible gold dust
and baking supplies)
www.michaels.com

Monin (rose syrup)
www.americas.monin.com

More than Gourmet
(veal jus or demi-glace)
www.morethangourmet.com

N.Y. Cake & Baking Dist.
(edible gold dust)
www.nycake.com

Russ & Daughters (gravlax)
www.russanddaughters.com

Scharffen Berger (artisan chocolate)
www.scharffenberger.com

The Sugar Diva (party goods
and baking supplies)
www.thesugardiva.com

Three Tarts (flavored marshmallows)
www.3tarts.com

Vermont Creamery (crème fraîche)
www.vermontcreamery.com

Vitamix (blenders)
www.vitamix.com

Williams-Sonoma (mail-order
pastries and Staub blue pots)
www.williamssonoma.com

HOME DÉCOR & FURNITURE

Adirondack chairs
www.adirondackchairs.com

B. D. Jeffries
www.bdjeffries.com

Custom Artisan Group (custom iron
work, including candelabras)
www.customartisangroup.com

Gracious Home
www.gracioushome.com

Gump's (silver trays)
www.gumps.com

M&J Trimming (ribbon)
www.mjtrim.com

Oscar de la Renta
www.oscardelarenta.com

Paper Lantern Store
(Chinese lanterns)
www.paperlanternstore.com

Ralph Lauren Home
(silver trays, wicker tray,
hurricanes, and tablecloths)
www.ralphlauren.com

Raymond Goins (fine furniture &
specialty paint finishing)
www.rlgoins.com

LINENS

Antique Linen
www.antiquelinen.com

Belle Chambre
www.bellechambre.com

Charlotte Moss (trade only)
www.charlottemoss.com

Colibri Textiles Dyeing
(tea-staining fabric)
38 West 32nd Street, Suite 1500
New York, NY 10001
212-967-0919

Cowtan & Tout (trade only)
www.cowtan.com

D. Porthault
www.dporthaultparis.com

Gracious Style
www.graciousstyle.com

Gramercy Fine Linens
and Furnishings
www.shopgramercy.com

Leontine Linens (Rollins monogram)
www.leontinelinens.com

Les Indiennes
www.lesindiennes.com

No. Four Eleven
(monogrammed linens)
www.numberfoureleven.com

Pierre Frey (trade only)
www.pierrefrey.com

Premier Burlap Table Linens
1-800-614-6185
www.burlap-tablecloth.com

Roberta Roller Rabbit
www.robertarollerrabbit.com

Schumacher (trade only)
www.fschumacher.com

Schweitzer Linen
www.schweitzerlinen.com

Sferra
www.sferra.com

Susan Shepherd Interiors (trade only)
904-241-5900

Travis & Company (trade only)
www.travisandcompany.com

Turkish Towel Store
www.turkishtowelstore.com

Valombreuse
www.valombreuse.fr

Walker Valentine Custom House
www.walkervalentine.com

PLACE CARDS, INVITATIONS & CALLIGRAPHY

Dempsey & Carroll
www.dempseyandcarroll.com

Gadabout Paper (hand-drawn cards)
www.agadabout.com

Ginna Dunlap Emmet Calligraphy
www.ginnadunlapemmetcalligraphy.com

Lala's Hand
(hand-painted place cards)
Laurie Howard
phoward796@aol.com

Mrs. John L. Strong
www.mrsstrong.com

Paces Papers, Inc., by Jackie
www.pacespapers.com

The Printery
www.iprintery.com

PLANTS & GARDEN ACCESSORIES

Boxwoods Gardens & Gifts
www.boxwoodsonline.com

Jamali Garden
www.jamaligarden.com

Lexington Gardens
(containers, vases, and pots)
www.lexingtongardensnyc.com

Lush Life Garden & Flowers
www.lushlifehomegarden.com

Treillage (leather coolers)
www.bunnywilliams.com/treillage

RESTAURANTS & CATERERS

Cardamom Hill
Chef: Asha Gomez
www.cardamomhill.net

Chef Julia LeRoy
chefjulialeroy.com
chefjulialeroy@gmail.com
www.chefjulialeroy.com

Dennis Dean Catering
www.dennisdeancatering.com

Farm Burger
Chef: Dan Latham
www.farmburger.net

Fig & Olive
www.figandolive.com

Holeman & Finch
www.holeman-finch.com

Kevin Rathbun Steak
(prime steakhouse)
Chef: Kevin Rathbun
www.kevinrathbunsteak.com

Krog Bar (Mediterranean tapas bar)
Chef: Kevin Rathbun
www.krogbar.com

KR SteakBar
Chef: Kevin Rathbun
www.kevinrathbun.com/kr-steakbar.html

La Esquina
Chef: Akhtar Nawab
www.esquinanyc.com

A Legendary Event
www.legendaryevents.com

Lenôtre Paris (caterer)
www.lenotre.com

Peachtree Road Farmers Market
www.peachtreeroadfarmersmarket.com

Rathbun's (modern American cuisine)
Chef: Kevin Rathbun
www.rathbunsrestaurant.com

Restaurant Eugene
Chef: Linton Hopkins
www.restauranteugene.com

Star Provisions
Bacchanalia, Abattoir, Quinones, Star
Provisions, and Floataway Café
Chef: Anne Quatrano
www.starprovisions.com

Yeah Burger
Chef: Shaun Doty
www.yeahburger.com

SILVER

Beverly Bremer Silver Shop
www.beverlybremer.com

H. G. Robertson Fine Silver & Gifts
www.hgrobertson.com

Silver Gallery (silver julep cups)
www.silvergallery.com

Wakefield-Scearce Galleries
(silver julep cups)
www.wakefieldscearce.com

TABLE ACCESSORIES

Horchow
(chinoiserie salt and pepper shakers)
www.horchow.com

Oriental Furniture (Asian fishbowls)
www.orientalfurniture.com

WINE & COCKTAILS

Aardvark (white paper straws)
www.aardvarkstraws.com

Blackbird Vineyards
www.blackbirdvineyards.com

Fee Brothers (bitters)
www.feebrothers.com

H&F Bottle Shop (specialty liquors)
www.hfbottleshop.com

Intoxicologist (cocktail recipes)
www.intoxicologist.net

pH Wine Merchant
www.phwinemerchant.com

Stéphane Bonnerot
(French sommelier)
CHATEAUX & SERVICES
011-33-1-55-92-57-32

OTHER

Chantecaille
www.chantecaille.com

Hudson Urban Bicycles
(custom bicycles)
www.hudsonurbanbicycles.com

Liberty Puzzles
www.libertypuzzles.com

Taffin (jewelry)
www.taffin.com

Verdura (jewelery)
www.verdura.com

United States Croquet Association
(to find an instructor near you)
www.croquetamerica.com

CONVERSION CHART
All conversions are approximate.

LIQUID CONVERSIONS

U.S.	METRIC
1 tsp	5 ml
1 tbs	15 ml
2 tbs	30 ml
3 tbs	45 ml
¼ cup	60 ml
⅓ cup	75 ml
⅓ cup + 1 tbs	90 ml
⅓ cup + 2 tbs	100 ml
½ cup	120 ml
⅔ cup	150 ml
¾ cup	180 ml
¾ cup + 2 tbs	200 ml
1 cup	240 ml
1 cup + 2tbs	275 ml
1 ¼ cups	300 ml
1 ⅓ cups	325 ml
1 ½ cups	350 ml
1 ⅔ cups	375 ml
1 ¾ cups	400 ml
1 ¾ cups + 2 tbs	450 ml
2 cups (*1 pint*)	475 ml
2 ½ cups	600 ml
3 cups	720 ml
4 cups (*1 quart*)	945 ml
	(*1,000 ml is 1 liter*)

WEIGHT CONVERSIONS

U.S./U.K.	METRIC
½ oz	14 g
1 oz	28 g
1 ½ oz	43 g
2 oz	57 g
2 ½ oz	71 g
3 oz	85 g
3 ½ oz	100 g
4 oz	113 g
5 oz	142 g
6 oz	170 g
7 oz	200 g
8 oz	227 g
9 oz	255 g
10 oz	284 g
11 oz	312 g
12 oz	340 g
13 oz	368 g
14 oz	400 g
15 oz	425 g
1 lb	454 g

OVEN TEMPERATURES

°F	GAS MARK	°C
250	½	120
275	1	140
300	2	150
325	3	165
350	4	180
375	5	190
400	6	200
425	7	220
450	8	230
475	9	240
500	10	260
550	Broil	290

ACKNOWLEDGMENTS

Aspecial thanks to my family and dearest friends:

My parents, Jan and Ron Deaton, especially my mom, for hours and hours and hours of proofreading and editing, and for encouraging me to follow my dreams, always, and for teaching me that "Life is 1 percent inspiration and 99 percent perspiration."

My children, Emerson, Carlyle, and Preston Rollins, for faithfully supporting me with their encouragement and patience and being my inspiration for living with grace (even if it is sometimes grace under pressure).

Emerson: for your rose de-thorning abilities and for being my heavy lifter, the muscles and brawn who keeps calm, cool, and collected with an always level head.

Carlyle: my "mini-me" junior editor and fashion stylist; your smiles and thoughtfulness brighten up any day.

Preston: my table setter, place-card placer, and chief encourager of using the "good stuff"; you keep me on my toes.

You make every day a soirée.

Glen Rollins, who made me realize that I could chase my dreams and find happiness at the end of the race. And that even when the door closes, the windows are still open.

My cordial coterie of blondes—Mary Johnson, Cynthia Hammond, Robin Howell, Nina Cheney, Ashley Dabbiere, and Ashley Preisinger—thank you all for keeping me blonde rather than gray!

Dennis Dean, my fellow in orange, for being at my side for every party and always being my biggest cheerleader.

Miles Redd, for pushing me to do this book, encouraging me to find happiness in other ways than paint colors, and introducing me to my agent. I thought you were crazy but it turned out to be the best SSRI a girl could ever have!

To my assortment of friends and supporters, including (but not limited to):

Leslie Podell, Paige Rustum, Margaret Caldwell, Molly Pastor, Amy Nelson, Graham Anthony, Ginny Brewer, Elizabeth Klump, Deborah Kelly, Rich Amons, Caroline Tucker, Ginny Tinley, Jeanne Hastings, Mickey Freeman, Harrison Rohr, Summer Tompkins Walker, Lulu Powers, Celerie Kemble, Jill Fairchild, Kate Wadley, Sallie Rothschild, Alex Hitz, Christina Murphy, Amanda Taylor, Sara Kennedy, Carolyn Englefield, Dominique Love, Carolyn Carr, Elizabeth Roth, Bunny Williams, Patrick McMullan, Mavis Humes Baird, Peg McCall Fiman, Sonia Dawson, Maria Sanchez, and the rest of you who have supported me through a particularly rough year and encouraged me to keep going. And going and going.

To those who keep me party ready:

Anna Pare, Lauren Bays, Kyle Moon, Mari Watkins, and Mirna Castillo.

To those who helped me host parties and/or honored me with the pleasure of their company:

Oscar de la Renta, Rachel Roy, Lela Rose and Brandon Jones, Emily Giffin, Miles Redd, David York, Cynthia and Brad Hammond, Robin and Hilton Howell, Ashley and Alan Dabbiere, Gil Schafer, Leslie Podell, Kimball Hastings/Ralph Lauren, Neiman Marcus of Atlanta, and Saks Fifth Avenue of Atlanta.

To the best chefs and food lovers, for your recipes and creativity:

Julia LeRoy, Shaun Doty, Linton Hopkins, Kevin Rathbun, Anne Quatrano, Asha Gomez, Pascal Lorange, Dennis Dean, Akhtar Nawab, Dan Latham, Kim Sunée, Drew Ihrig, and to all of the servers who kept the drinks filled and the wines flowing, and for their always attentive service.

To my publishing and promotion team:

Jill Cohen, my agent and den mother, for believing

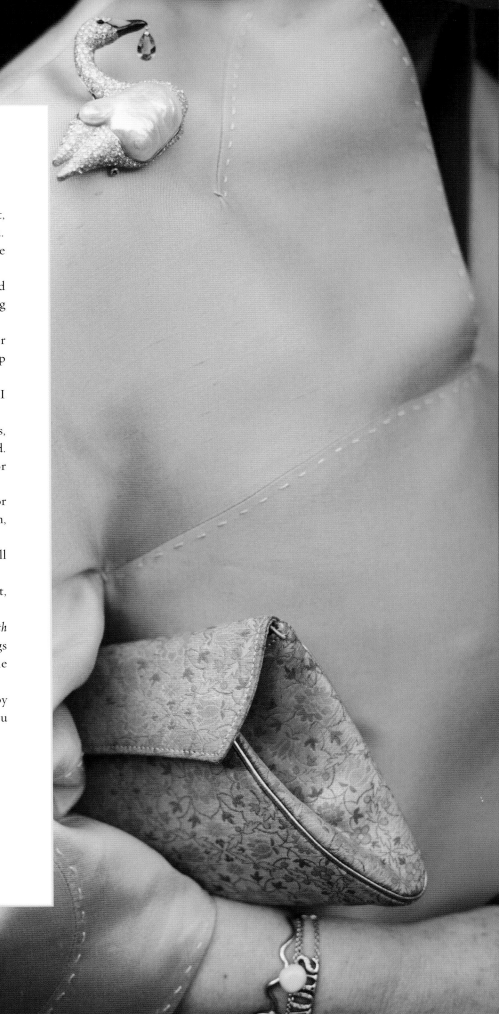

in me despite my being "a nobody," and her assistant, Sam Kopf. I could have never done this without you.

Ellen Rubin, my publicist, for working to help me become "a somebody."

Doug Turshen, for his beautiful book design, and his associate Steve Turner. Julia Turshen, for helping me early on, getting my feet wet!

Charles Miers and Kathleen Jayes of Rizzoli, for publishing my book and working so diligently to help me achieve this dream.

Dara Caponigro of *Veranda*, for recognizing that I had a gift and encouraging me to use it.

Alan Kauffman and Stephen Strick, my attorneys, for helping me negotiate all the stuff I don't understand.

Nancy Staab and Stephanie Kirkorkian, for tweaking my writing in all the right places.

Rob Crigler, the domain guru, and Jenette Lee, for the beautiful Web design of www.danielledrollins.com, and Aditya Sunchu, for making the design a reality.

To the talented photographers who captured all of the best moments:

John Kernick, Quentin Bacon, Julie Skarratt, Sarah Dorio, and Philip Shone.

To everyone who has carried *Soirée: Entertaining with Style*, promoted the book, and hosted book signings and enthusiastically encouraged their friends to come to them!

And finally, to all my friends who are my happy companions on "The Sown Oats Book Tour"—you know who you are and how I feel about you!

RECIPE INDEX

PHOTOGRAPHY CREDITS

1 John Kernick

2 John Kernick

3 Julie Skarratt

4 John Kernick

5 Quentin Bacon

6-7 Quentin Bacon

8 -9 Sarah Dorio

10 Quentin Bacon

11 John Kernick

12 John Kernick

13 Julie Skarratt

14-15 John Kernick

16-33 Quentin Bacon

34- 47 John Kernick

48-59 John Kernick

60-77 John Kernick

78-85 John Kernick

86- 99 John Kernick

100-111 John Kernick

112-125 John Kernick

126-135 John Kernick

136-149 Quentin Bacon

150-154 Sarah Dorio

155 Clockwise from top left:
Philip Shone, Sarah Dorio,
Sarah Dorio, Philip Shone,
Philip Shone, Sarah Dorio,

156 Sarah Dorio

157 John Kernick

158 Sarah Dorio

159 Sarah Dorio

160 From left to right:
Philip Shone, John Kernick,
Sarah Dorio

161 John Kernick

162-163 John Kernick

164-177 John Kernick

178 -195 Quentin Bacon

196 -209 Quentin Bacon

209 John Kernick

210 -230 Quentin Bacon

231 John Kernick

236-237 John Kernick

238 -239 Quentin Bacon

First published in the United States of America in 2012
by Rizzoli International Publications, Inc.
300 Park Avenue South
New York, NY 10010
www.rizzoliusa.com

2015 2016 2017 2018 / 10 9 8 7 6 5

Distributed in the U.S. trade by Random House, New York

Printed in China

ISBN-13: 978-0-8478-3873-8

Library of Congress Catalog Control Number: 2012936358

Art Direction: Doug Turshen with Steve Turner